EXOTIC PLANTING
for
Adventurous
Gardeners

Christopher Lloyd
& friends

Photographs by
Jonathan Buckley

Edited by
Erica Hunningher

Exotic
Planting

for
Adventurous
Gardeners

ER PRESS

Half title page *Fergus Garrett and Matt Reese wrestle with a prickly pear that has spent the summer outside and now, at the beginning of November, needs to be lifted for overwintering under frost-free glass.*

Title page *The Exotic Garden in early August. A rich mixture of foliage plants includes* Colocasia esculenta, Butia capitata, Pennisetum setaceum *'Rubrum'*, Musa basjoo *and* Ricinus communis *'New Zealand Purple', with dahlias, cannas and* Verbena bonariensis *adding pizzazz.*

CONTENTS

Frank Ronan

PREFACE

Somewhere, and I wish I could find it, Christo once wrote of wanting to make a tropical border at Dixter. He described a sort of island bed and wondered where to put it...

I REMEMBER, in the early days of our friendship, reading that and writing to point out that the rose garden was the ideal site for his vision. I don't think that I can have been the only person to make the suggestion, and he must have thought of it himself anyway every time he was snagged by one of the antediluvian brutes that grimly hung on in that corner of Dixter, up to their knees in grass clippings. His response was that the idea was good, but who would have the energy to undertake such a project?

The answer, eventually, was Fergus Garrett, who became head gardener at Dixter in 1993. That year the gaps among the roses were plugged with *Canna indica* 'Purpurea', as a kind of tentative preamble. The following March most of the old roses were ripped out. Christo recorded: 'The rending noise of huge old roots reminded me of a hyena devouring a plank of wood.' At the time his palette of replacements was surprisingly (to us, now) limited: 'I have as yet only unformulated ideas of what will be included, aside from cannas, the verbena, castor oil plants, perhaps dahlias, *Melianthus major* (of course). There are quite a lot of seeds I ordered....' What I remember of that year is mostly an overwhelming haze of 'the verbena', *V. bonariensis*. But even that was enough to make what had been the dullest part of Dixter into the most exciting.

At first he insisted on calling it 'The Old Rose Garden'. I tried to persuade him to use that as the title of this book, but he would only take a joke so far. He said that he was in enough trouble with the rose people as it was. Which somehow undermines the prevalent idea that Christo, above all, loved to shock. An idea so accepted that it is stated, with affection, by several contributors to this book. I can't say that I knew him better, but I know that shock was not his intention. He might have enjoyed the overreaction of others, but that was never what he set out to achieve. Who would go to the enormous trouble of making an exotic garden only to see dismay on the faces of people you thought little of anyway? No, he made that garden out of an absolute love of the plants and the desire to grow them. If there had been no-one else to look at it, or be shocked, he (and Fergus) would have done it all the same.

When Christo died he left some big gaps behind him. The strength of his personality made the world seem a hollow place in his absence. One of the physical gaps he left was this book, incomplete, yet with enough material set down to make us want to finish it on his behalf. When Fergus asked me if I would take on the project, refusal was not an option. Friendship with Christo worked on the basis that you do whatever you can for your friends, without question. It was one of the principles that made us friends in the first place.

Also, I felt partly responsible. The day that Christo finished the manuscript for *Succession Planting for Adventurous Gardeners* I spoke to Fergus on the phone, and he, ever thinking of Christo, said, 'Now I've got to get him started on the next book, but I don't know what it should be about.' I said it was obvious it should be about the Exotic Garden, and Fergus agreed. A week later, Christo and I were driving through Scotland on our annual jaunt, when he said that he didn't know what book he was going to do next. 'Exotic,' I said, 'and Fergus thinks so too.'

That settled it, somehow. Making suggestions is no trouble at all, and I thought no more about it until some eighteen months later, in the middle of grief— and the worst thing about grief is the feeling that there is nothing you can do—I was given something to do. The only snag was, when I eventually got hold of the manuscript, that there wasn't quite enough material for me to work on. I could amend and append, always with Christo's voice in my ear, but it wouldn't be enough. It was time to call on some of the other friends.

The gardening world is small, in reality. The garden writing world is minuscule. Most of the people who know their subject and write well had been Christo's friends. We had a rich well to draw from—many more than we had room for. And, not surprisingly, there was a great willingness to help. To know Christo had been to feel indebted to him.

So, what we have here is Christopher Lloyd's last work, unfinished, but still worth reading for everyone who loved reading him. We also have, I hope, what he intended us to have: a complete book on the subject of the Exotic Garden, by a variety of authors who are foremost in their field.

Thank you to Anna Pavord, who was the first person I asked for help, not least because, as she is the wisest and most scrupulous among garden writers, I needed her blessing before the project could get under way. She has written a piece about the history of the exotic garden that accomplishes the great feat of being both scholarly and compelling.

Thank you to Roy Lancaster, whose breadth of knowledge is astonishing. He has brought to this book the confident stride of a writer who has walked among exotics in the wild as well as knowing them in cultivation.

Thank you to Dan Hinkley, who also brings an intrepid air with him. That gives an irresistible gloss to his qualification to be the best person to tell us all we need to know about big leaves.

Thank you to Andrew Lawson. With his photographer's eye he has given us the benefit of his intimacy with colour.

Thank you to Stephen Anderton, who has evoked what it is to be among exotic plants, in the Lloydian sense.

Thank you to Ray Waite, whose detailed knowledge of *Begonia* and *Coleus* has been an embellishment to this book.

Thank you to Tom Cooper, whom I kept in reserve until the last moment, knowing that there would be a gap and that he would be the man to fill it, with consummate professionalism and integrity. His piece about pot displays betrays nothing of the cruelly short

notice I gave him to write it. Thank you to Tim Miles, who has furnished us with specialist knowledge of edible exotics in pots.

Thank you to Mary Keen, not only for taking on the daunting task of writing a devil's advocate piece, and doing it brilliantly, but for being an ally throughout. Her humour and good sense were what carried me through several crises.

Thank you to Helen Dillon, who agreed to the most troublesome task of all. She compiled the plant directory. What might have been drudgery was transformed into pleasure as we sat in her house in Dublin for two days, laughing and gossiping our way through the alphabet of plants (I should also thank Val Dillon, who oiled my wheels during this process with his best Sancerre).

Lastly, thanks to Tony Lord, who made the essential contribution of checking plant nomenclature.

▲ *Christo with his 'great confederate', Fergus Garrett—a meeting of minds that made, and continues to make, the Exotic Garden the most exciting part of Dixter.*

The call of
THE EXOTIC

Early in the morning or before the sun goes down are my favourite times in the Exotic Garden. The colours are crisper in the low light, and there's the peace and quiet of out of hours. I am never bored or tired of this space — it fills my veins with adrenalin.

The very idea of an exotic garden is a direct invitation for a good wallow. Gone all asceticism and self-denial. From the first, it is intended to indulge. We shall have to work for this outcome but the rewards are beckoning.

Just the word exotic conjures up visions of the bizarre. To me it means something beautiful, colourful, curious, full of mystery, an alien world that we walk into and are transported to peculiar and unfamiliar surroundings. It gives us the excuse to do something outlandish, to splash out, and be freer than ever. This way of gardening is not everyone's cake but I love every bit of it. When mine is in full swing from August onwards I am drawn to it. My route to another part of the garden will always be through this exotic world.

Exoticism originates out there, abroad. It applies to warmer countries, or at least to countries with warmer summers than ours. We wouldn't seek it in Greenland or Siberia, but most certainly in warm temperate, even subtropical countries, where moisture and warmth between them promote an enviable lushness in the vegetation.

Why can't I have something like that? we ask ourselves. Why not, indeed? I am fortunate enough to have the framework of Dixter to work in, and the old rose garden is the perfect site for a little piece of make-believe, enclosed by yew hedges and by the hovel — an ancient cow house — on the northern side. The original plan was designed by Edwin Lutyens in 1912. But, you don't need a Dixter to have this sort of fun. My head gardener Fergus Garrett has for years experimented with his pocket handkerchief courtyard in Old Town Hastings with a good deal of success. Will Giles does it well in Norwich, Kingston Maurward College have been doing it for years in Dorset, and so has Ray Waite at the Royal Horticultural Society Garden, Wisley.

◄ *On steamy mornings in high summer you can feel—almost hear—the plants revelling in the high humidity of the sort of weather that makes many people gasp, 'This is too much,' and fan themselves languidly with yesterday's newspaper.*

▶ An aerial view of Dixter, showing the gardens lying round the house and the rose garden protected by the hovel and yew hedges. The site is some 16 kilometres or 10 miles from the coast, 55m/180ft above sea level, and slopes down to the Rother valley. Shelter belts of trees filter the wind on all sides.

▶ The rose garden seen from the roof of the house in the winter of 1924. The original plan, 'prettily shaped, architectural yet not unduly formal', was designed by Edwin Lutyens on the site of a farm cattle yard and includes a circular, brick, cattle-drinking tank. There are scalloped yew hedges on three sides and an ancient cow house—the hovel—on the fourth. The geometrically shaped beds are divided by flagstone paving.

▶ The rose garden designed by Lutyens in 1912 had ten geometric beds, each planted with Hybrid Teas introduced around the turn of the century, all in shades of pink: in beds 1 and 2 'Viscountess Folkestone', with creamy silvery-pink flowers, 1886; shell pink 'La Tosca', 1901, in beds 3 and 4; 'Prince de Bulgarie', 1900, with silvery flesh-coloured flowers, shaded salmon and saffron yellow; in beds 7 and 8 'Madame Abel Chatenay', 1895, pale pink flowers with deeper pink centres and reverse carmine-pink; and in 9 and 10 'Earl of Warwick', 1904, with flowers a pale pinkish buff and livid pink on the reverse.

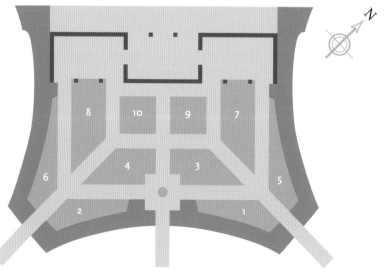

▶ The rose garden in summer, in the 1920s, with Daisy Lloyd by the cattle-drinking tank. The oldest roses were brought to Dixter by Nathaniel and Daisy Lloyd from their first garden (they were married in 1905). The beds are edged with pinks.

GREAT DIXTER. THE ROSE GARDEN. 6023.

▶ The rose garden in 1980, still full of roses, although there were plans afoot for diversification. 'I am not keen on rose gardens consisting only of roses,' Christopher wrote some ten years later. 'Eventually, mine may end by having none at all! At any rate, I am diversifying.'

▶ In 1995, a few roses remain, including the creamy pink 'Chanelle' in the fore-ground, but the old rose garden has been transformed and is in its third year. The tender is mixed with the hardy, but always with a sense of lush flamboyance. There are cannas, with their splendid leaves and silken flowers, brilliant dahlias, exciting foliage plants including Yucca gloriosa and Phormium 'Sundowner', and Verbena bonariensis running riot to create a linking theme. Over the years, the Exotic Garden has become richer in shape and texture.

▶▶ The view from the roof that echoes the 1924 photograph (opposite, centre) but the year is 2005 and the Exotic Garden is in full swing.

In the 1980s Jimmy Hancock was giving a subtropical flavour to the borders
at Powis Castle (I wrote about them in *Other People's Gardens*) with cannas,
dahlias, arundo, melianthus and stooled paulownias.

So with a little effort, a little climatic cooperation, and a little daring, it's
there within our grasp. Not every summer is dismal, after all, but it's up to us
to be ready to seize our opportunities when, unannounced, they materialize.
And even if the summers do not cooperate, you can achieve a degree of
exoticism by using perfectly hardy plants that have an exotic look. Bamboos,
fatsias, large-leaved bergenias and hostas, the spikes of yuccas and irises, and
ferns of all sorts, go some way to giving you that look.

Big, lush leaves and strong shapes are what I imagined to form the bones
of my Exotic Garden. Shapes are everything, but colour is also important. No
pastel shades for me here but instead dazzling reds, oranges and magenta
from cannas and dahlias. I didn't want to restrict myself to any group of
plants but to try anything and everything. Some plants are bone hardy whilst
others can barely stand a degree of frost. This is not everybody's idea of a
tropical garden, especially as only a few of my ingredients are truly tropical.
The mix of hardy through to tender works for me at Dixter. Give me a hotter
climate then perhaps I would lean heavily on other plants.

And some plants are full of surprises. Be aware of your microclimates,
not only in your area but also around your property. Fergus gets away with
murder on the coast in Hastings only 17 kilometres or 11 miles from here.
I wouldn't dream of getting *Begonia luxurians* through a winter (even the

mildest Dixter winter) unprotected here, but he does (although the plant looks miserable). A metropolis like London will be quite a few degrees warmer than us. Also, the protection of a wall, or the comfort of a heating duct, a dry area snug right up against a house or greenhouse, will make all the difference.

Drainage matters too because in many cases it's the wet that kills and not the low temperatures. Tim Miles of Cotswold Wildlife Park uses all sorts of plants outside that we wouldn't dream of risking, but he has sharp drainage and uses hardier varieties. A few plants are lost on the way but we all learn from these mistakes.

LEARNING TO BE EXOTIC

When I visited a nature reserve on the southern shore of Lake Michigan, near Chicago, what should be my astonishment when I saw wild opuntias flourishing in the sand. You know, those prickly pear things. How could they stand the savage winters? Perhaps just a question of acquiring the right opuntia and giving it, as far as possible, the conditions it would enjoy.

Another opuntia example, again from the USA. On the sloping roof of a lean-to extension, David Culp (better known for his hellebores, but I have yet to join the hellebore bores) had established a colony of this cactus. It looked weird but wonderful, providing a touch of surrealism. Surely that should not be too difficult to emulate. We already, in Britain, see ferns colonizing roofs on drippy north aspects and fascinating they are, but opuntias on the roof's sunny side would make a change.

When I was in Nairobi some years ago (1945, to be precise!), beneath trees in a public garden, blocks of flamboyant cannas were bedded out. I was greatly struck by this and have been a canna addict ever since, even lending a hand in promoting their cause in England. In a bad summer they can be a bit of a flop, one has honestly to admit, their blooms turning to a brown mush, but far from always is it like that. When we see them flaunting, it transports us into another world.

Being sensible makes sense, but how boring to be relentlessly sensible all the time. I remember how it used to enrage my sister when my mother told her she should wear sensible shoes or a sensible hat. Any gardener having a spark in them should enjoy a spirit of adventure from time to time and that is not necessarily sensible. We get carried along, carried away and although there are attendant anxieties, there are also stabs of exhilaration which must not be denied. After all, as a friend once said to me apropos of a husband she'd had for three blissful years but who turned out to be a wrong'n, a fool's paradise is better than no paradise at all.

We learn from our mistakes, so our gardening does improve all the time but without necessarily becoming safer. We are always on the borderlines of what it's sensible to attempt. Such gardening may be silly but it may, on the other hand, be the most exciting.

▼ *Mexican* Opuntia robusta *is a prickly pear with big, Mickey-Mouse-like pads and barbed bristles. The pads face in different directions, catching the light in varied ways, so that there is a great play of light and shade.*

▲ A gap in the yew hedges that enclose the Exotic Garden on three sides (the fourth, on the northern side, has the hovel) is an invitation to enter another world, to plunge through lush vegetation and, on misty mornings, to be enveloped in jungle vapour. The vegetation encloses you, but only up to head height and a little beyond, and never so high as to block out sunlight. A real jungle would be rather too overpowering and threatening.

CLIMATE CHANGE?

What, if anything, is this climate change we keep hearing of all about? It is hard to tell when there are so many contrary views. All that gardeners need to know is how it affects them. Whether the warming up is temporary or permanent, we need to take advantage of its plus values. That's where the exotic garden comes in. We have an area of shelter, where the wind blows less, for in this country at least, wind is the great enemy, far more than frost. Warm, sheltered sites also have a way of being frost pockets but that may well matter less than you might think.

I must say a word about pessimism and optimism. As a safeguard against nemesis, most people tend to be pessimistic. At the backs of their minds they have the primitive notion that punishment awaits those who take a rosy view of life. This is all mixed up with religion or superstition. The 'touch wood' approach to life. If we are pessimistic, no one can accuse us of having been caught out. If, for instance, someone with a supposed flair for prognosis declares that the omens indicate a hard winter ahead, the seer will be taken notice of. If it turns out to be a mild winter after all, the mistake will pass unnoticed. But the same seer will never be caught out predicting a mild winter. Oh no. If that turned out to be wrong, he would lose all credibility.

We may yet, perhaps quite soon, be able accurately to predict the climate or weather as much as six months ahead on scientific grounds and we do better in this respect than we did, but for my part I still think it is best to take what precautions, ahead of winter, that I think are sensible without going over the top about them so that winter becomes a season to dread, inconvenient though it inevitably is, and disease-promoting for us humans. Plants are not humans. My point is that the spot which is cosy and conducive, with a bit of help from us, to lush plant growth may, by the very nature of its position, also be a frost pocket; indeed the coldest spot in your winter garden. But this doesn't matter. By the time winter arrives your tender plants will be safely provided for in one way or another until the following June, when their temporarily frost-prone nook will be cosy again.

When we think about exotica, we need to realize that their requirements may vary widely under the care we give them in the limited space that we can offer. It is the difference between cacti and similar succulents, and plants like begonias, say, used to abundant moisture during their growing season. We can cope with both, I do believe, but it requires a bit of organization. Sun and shade are important factors that need dealing with as best we can. In June, when the sun's declination is at its highest, it may be quite difficult to provide shade at midday, but there'll be more to say on that when I write about June planting out (page 150). Before getting down to practical details I just want to emphasize once more the great feeling of involvement which exotic gardening gives, the feeling of being part of and wrapped into a voluptuous, living community. There's plenty of work attached but from the results you need to be able to say with conviction, I enjoyed that.

PLAN OF THE EXOTIC GARDEN SHOWING HARDY AND STRUCTURAL INGREDIENTS

▼ *Though liable to get cut to the ground in winter, Tetrapanax papyrifer is hardier than you think and will sprout again each spring.*

▼▼ *The giant reed grass, Arundo donax, makes a bold focal feature in the circular brick cattle-drinking tank.*

▶▶ Top: *The huge, wide furry leaves of a stooled Paulownia tomentosa. Below: The juvenile foliage of* Eucalyptus gunnii *is small and rounded and very blue.*

Arundo donax in cattle drinking tank

BED 1
Dicksonia antarctica (*Da*)
Dryopteris erythrosora (*D*)
Acer negundo 'Flamingo' (*A*)
Hedychium forrestii (*H*)
Yucca flaccida 'Ivory' (*Y*)

BED 2
Miscanthus sinensis 'Variegatus' (*M*)
Rosa 'Madge' (*RM*)
Paulownia tomentosa (*Pt*)

BED 3
Rosa 'Ballerina' (*RB*)
Musa basjoo (*Mb*)
Tetrapanax papyrifer (*T*)
Eucalyptus gunnii (*Eg*)
Kniphofia caulescens (*Kc*)

BED 4
Eucalyptus gunnii (*Eg*)
Tetrapanax papyrifer (*T*)
Phormium 'Sundowner' (*PS*)
Rosa 'Chanelle' (*RC*)
Polystichum polyblepharum (*Pp*)

BED 5
Sophora 'Little Baby' (*S*)
Arundo donax (*A*)

BED 6
Euphorbia donii (*Ed*)
Phormium cookianum subsp. hookeri
  'Tricolor' (*PchT*)
Pseudopanax ferox (*Pf*)
Amicia zygomeris (*Az*)

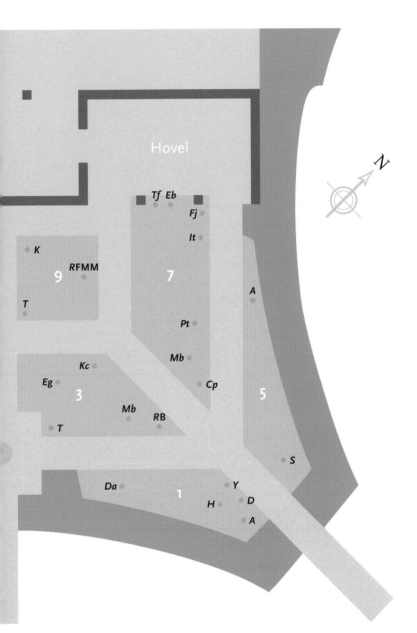

BED 7
Musa basjoo (*Mb*)
Paulownia tomentosa (*Pt*)
Impatiens tinctoria (*It*)
Escallonia bifida (*Eb*)
Farfugium japonicum 'Argenteum' (*Fj*)
Trachycarpus fortunei (*Tf*)
Calopsis paniculata (*Cp*)

BED 8
Musa basjoo (*Mb*)
Solanum laxum 'Album' (*SlA*)
Clematis 'Niobe' (*CN*)
Ailanthus altissima (*Aa*)
Phormium (*P*)
Eucalyptus gunnii (*Eg*)
Euphorbia mellifera (*Em*)
Clematis 'Madame Julia Correvon' (*CMJC*)
Clematis 'Marcel Moser' (*CMM*)

BED 9
Tetrapanax papyrifer (*T*)
Rosa 'Florence Mary Morse'
  (*RFMM*)
Kniphofia linearifolia (*K*)

BED 10
Rosa 'Mrs Oakley Fisher' (*RMOF*)
Eucalyptus gunnii (*Eg*)
Yucca gloriosa (*Yg*)
Dicksonia squarrosa (*Ds*)
Melianthus major (*Mm*)
Thalia dealbata (*Td*)
Fuchsia 'Mr West' (*FMW*)
Fuchsia 'Lena' (*FL*)
Farfugium japonicum 'Argenteum'
  (*Fj*)
Tetrapanax papyrifer (*T*)

Anna Pavord

AN EXOTIC PAST

When Christopher planted tropical bananas, cannas and castor oil plants in his Edwardian rose garden at Great Dixter, it was new and daring — almost sacrilegious — even though exotic gardens were the height of fashion in the latter part of the 19th century.

LOOKING BACK over the history of gardening in Britain, we tend to tell the story in aesthetic terms — one mode of beauty succeeding another as tastes changed. But, underpinning the aesthetics, there was usually a practical catalyst. The landscape park of the 18th century, for example, wasn't just a matter of an Englishman's dream of classical Italy. The dream could be paid for by the fact that the rents for grassland were high. In the mid-19th century a taste for exotic gardening in the tropical style hit Britain. You can read this as a reaction to the fashion of the previous century, but the style was driven by the fact that, for the first time, glass was cheap. Exotic plants need frost-free shelter during the winter and, without suitable winter quarters, wild, jungle displays of bananas and caladiums could not have arrived in the late-summer borders of Victorian Britain.

The change began around 1832 when Lucas Chance of Birmingham introduced into England a new method of blowing glass in cylinders. The technique was already being used in Germany and France. The Chance brothers saw that, with the new process, they could make glass in much bigger sheets than before. The new sheets were three feet long and ten inches wide (88 by 25cm), more than a foot longer than anything they had previously produced. Then, in 1845, the tax on glass was abolished and it became much cheaper to build the glasshouses in which gardeners could overwinter the great sub-tropical beasts of the exotic garden. During the next twenty years the price of glass fell to one fifth of its previous cost and the Chances' great moment came when 300,000 panes of their new glass were used to clad the great glasshouse that housed the Great Exhibition in Hyde Park in 1851.

There were improvements in heating too. The open fires used in the 18th century had produced a dry heat, entirely suitable for the plants then being introduced from the Cape. Tropicals needed something altogether damper and, eventually, gardeners found that hot water pipes running underground in a glasshouse that could be regularly damped-down provided a much better growing environment. But, at first, plants were often kept far too hot; rather than freezing to death, they were fried. The Scottish nurseryman Robert Ker (1816–1886) thought that 'forcing of any kind being an outrage done to nature, the more we avoid it the greater will be our success. She should be kindly assisted, not spurred nor thwarted when it can be avoided.'

FOREIGN PLANTS

Another catalyst in the business of growing exotic plants was the famous Wardian case, a mini-greenhouse on a wooden base, introduced by Nathaniel Bagshaw Ward in 1833. Ward was a physician who practised in the East End of London, but he was also a keen naturalist. In 1829 he sealed a chrysalis in a glass jar so that he could study its gradual transmogrification. But he also noticed how well some stray seedlings were growing in the humid, sealed-up environment of the jar, safe from gas fumes and desiccating draughts. Ward built an experimental series of larger containers and then, in 1836, published his findings in *The Companion To The Botanical Magazine*. The Wardian case meant that plant collectors, such as Robert Fortune, could bring in plants from China, Japan and India

▲ *On a misty August morning, Pseudopanax silhouetted against the house conjures a world far away from East Sussex.*

with a far greater chance of success. Lashed on the foredeck of sailing ships, these glass-topped cases kept plants safe from the dangers of salt spray, and with practically no need for watering. For the first time, thanks to the Wardian case, living plants could be transported long distances by sea.

By their very nature, of course, the kind of plants that were planted in the exotic garden were strange, unusual, wondrous. And foreign. The first banana plants to shiver their way through a British summer had been brought in from Assam and Japan. Phormiums came from New Zealand, tree ferns from Australia, cannas from Asia and the tropics of South America, castor oil plants (*Ricinus communis*) from Africa, agaves from Mexico, purple-leaved perilla from India, huge arrow-shaped caladiums from the West Indies. The idea of the exotic in itself was not new. Orange trees were exotic to the 17th century gardeners clever enough to get hold of them and rich enough to build glass-fronted orangeries in which they could overwinter.

Bedding out with exotic flowers was all the rage in the early part of the 19th century, using the zinnias that had arrived from Mexico in 1796, scarlet *Salvia splendens* that followed in 1822, and *Begonia semperflorens* that came in from Brazil in 1829. Nor was the general idea of plunging tender exotics in the open ground during summer a new notion. Philip Miller (1691–1771) was doing this during his time as curator of the Chelsea Physic Garden, but for the plants' sake rather than the gardeners'. It gave over-wintered exotics a chance to recuperate from life in a fume-filled greenhouse. It also gave the gardeners a chance to clean the glass.

SUBTROPICAL FOLIAGE

From the 1860s onwards there was a marked shift away from the exotic flower bedding that had obsessed the previous generation of gardeners towards a greater use of subtropical foliage plants. In effect this was still bedding, but now mountains of the castor oil plant, *Ricinus communis*, towered above the parterre at Maiden Bradley in Wiltshire. Yuccas and exotic palm trees appeared at Linton Park, the home of the Cornwallis family near Maidstone, Kent. Gardeners liked these foliage plants because they had a longer season in the garden. They were more resistant to rain than flowers were; the colours were subtler and the overall form of the plants much stronger. Rex begonias, dieffenbachias and philodendrons began to appear in beds, alongside hardier subjects such as bamboo and pampas.

This new style had been practised in mainland Europe for at least ten years before it appeared in Britain. Joseph Paxton (1803–1865), head gardener to the Duke of Devonshire at Chatsworth, noticed it in Germany, where he was travelling in 1852. 'Whole parterres and clumps are planted solely to exhibit specimens of foliage,' he wrote. 'I think much might be done in this country with the same object... Among the different plants ... the *Ficus elastica* appears to be the favourite; the *Canna indica, C. discolor* and especially the New Zealand flax.... There is a large *Caladium* much used in these parterres ... and *Maranta zebrina* from the stove appears to stand out for the summer.'

At the newly reconstructed Parc Monceau in Paris, Jean-Charles-Adolphe Alphand (1817–1891) and plantsman Jean-Pierre Barillet-Deschamps (1824–1875) worked together from 1855 onwards, experimenting enthusiastically with planting schemes using tender tropical and subtropical plants. Favourite centrepieces were tree ferns and bananas, unfolding over yuccas, agaves, caladiums, cannas and phormiums planted underneath. All, of course, had to be brought inside for the winter. Coloured foliage was much in demand: perilla, dark amaranthus and variegated coleus.

William Robinson, then working as gardening correspondent for *The Times*, visited Parc Monceau in 1867 and described the French way of packing low-growing plants like collars around big 'dot' plants: *Lobelia × speciosa* in a pool under the variegated giant reed, *Arundo donax* var. *versicolor*, mignonette carpeting the ground under the India rubber plant (*Ficus elastica*), the blue and white flowers of the Swan River daisy (*Brachyscome*) mingling under the handsome hairy leaves of a wigandia (*W. caracasana*) from Venezuela, a strap-leaved dragon tree (*Dracaena draco*) rearing out of a sea of coleus, a banana fringed with variegated tradescantia. Dahlias and cannas added a late-summer boost to the display of massed caladiums, their arrow-shaped leaves splashed in cream and pink and green. Robinson, associated now with the very different ideas expressed in *The Wild Garden* (1870), thought the style splendid and recommended that it be 'grandly used in the most formal of gardens laid out on the ordinary massing system'. In 1871 he published a book on *The Subtropical Garden*, in which he explained how similar effects could be achieved with hardy plants.

Meanwhile, in 1864 the Parc Monceau look had already spread to Battersea Park in London, where John Gibson (1815–1875) was the superintendent. Using the shelter provided by boundary trees and evergreen shrubberies, Gibson planted tree ferns, mop-headed dragon trees and wigandias in specially prepared planting pits. In order to provide perfect drainage and

extra warmth round the roots, the Battersea Park gardeners dug holes 30cm/1ft deep and built up the soil round each hole. They lined the pits with broken bricks to retain heat and then covered the bricks with turf laid upside-down to give a slow supply of nitrogen-rich humus. Like modern-day storage heaters, the bricks absorbed warmth during the day and released it at night. As late summer turned to autumn, this helped reduce the risk of early ground frosts harming the plants.

CANNAS AND OTHER SHOWY SUBJECTS

Though the new fashion was led by the experiments in the parks of Paris, it also depended on the work of early plant breeders, especially those who devoted themselves to showy subjects such as the South American canna. Cannas had been grown as stove-house plants since the beginning of the 19th century but, in 1846, a retired French consul at Valparaiso in Chile began hybridizing them to produce forms with bolder, more dramatic foliage. By 1856 he was crossing these hybrids with scarlet-flowered species to produce plants that had flowers just as brilliant as their leaves. His stock was distributed to French nurserymen and, with their salsa colours and fearless form, cannas became one of the most important elements in French displays of exotics. When they reached Britain they got an equally enthusiastic reception.

In an article on 'Planting our Subtropical and other Handsome-Foliaged Plants' which appeared in *The Journal of Horticulture* in 1866, Robert Fish, head gardener at Putteridge Bury Park in Bedfordshire, praised cannas in 'innumerable forms bearing bright flowers peeping through the foliage, some of which grew to five feet [1.5m] or more in height'. Fish also recommended gladioli and the castor oil plant, its huge leaves doused with reddish-purple, to mix with the cannas. Not all the plants he used were tender. As he pointed out, the Japanese *Hosta sieboldiana* was perfectly hardy but it had an exotic air and provided a useful contrast between taller castor oil plants.

Gardeners who had big beds to fill favoured plants that could be easily propagated. The castor oil plant was easy from seed sown in February or March. Plants

◀ *Castor oil,* Ricinus communis *'Carmencita', and* Cosmos bipinnatus *'Dazzler' in the Long Border at Dixter, with canna foliage in the background.*

▲ Canna *'Wyoming', which Christopher considered to be the finest of all orange cannas.*

would then be ready to set out in late May or early June, after all danger of frost had passed. Cannas could be overwintered under cover, just like dahlia tubers, the stems and leaves cut down and the roots packed away, safe from mice, in boxes of slightly damp compost.

In sheltered areas, glossy *Fatsia japonica* was hardy enough to overwinter out of doors. Gradually, gardeners also discovered that spiky yuccas were less tender than they looked, although their home was in the warm southern states of America. Dracaenas which came from Guinea and the Congo required careful overwintering, though the dragon tree, *Dracaena draco*, from the Canary Islands, was more forgiving. The wigandia from Caracas grew so rapidly it could be propagated each year from root cuttings, so space did not have to be found for it to overwinter.

▲ *Under the flapping sails* of Musa basjoo *and the huge leaves of* Tetrapanax papyrifer, *colourful dahlias, 'David Howard' and 'Bishop of Llandaff', appear like exotic birds in the jungle.*

Many hands were needed to manhandle bananas and palms under cover when the time came to dismantle the showy displays and prepare for winter. Henry Cooke, who made an exotic garden in Gloucestershire after serving as Surgeon General with the army in India, said he had to hire six men to get his banana trees under cover. The plants were loaded in turn on to a wooden sledge and dragged by a team of carthorses to his glasshouses, half a kilometre or 550 yards away.

THE SUBTROPICAL STYLE

In England, Gibson was generally acknowledged to be the king of gardening in the subtropical style. As a young man he had worked under Paxton at Chatsworth and had been sent to India to search for new rarities to enhance the Chatsworth collection, which was one of the best in Britain. At Battersea Park he tried to recreate scenes he remembered from his days in India: a 'cool and tropical forest scene' where beds of cannas mixed with other subtropical foliage plants. In one 'picturesque nook' was a huge Abyssinian banana (*Ensete ventricosum,* syn. *Musa ensete*) with leaves nearly 3.6m/12ft long, each billowing out from a bright red midrib. Fern Hollow was filled with a forest of tree ferns and palms with great coils of the Swiss cheese plant, *Monstera deliciosa* (more commonly seen cooped up in a pot), trained round the trunks. Huge staghorn ferns, *Platycerium bifurcatum,* from Australia, were wired on to stumps, the great antler-leaves rearing from the surrounding moss in a realistic approximation of their natural habitat. The subtropical garden became one of the park's chief attractions, glowingly described in the *Journal of Horticulture* in 1864 and 1865.

The style was appropriate only for reasonably sheltered gardens. Banana plants quickly looked tattered if they were planted in too exposed a site. At Putteridge Bury, Robert Fish tried to overcome the problems of an open, rather windy site, by laying out a small subtropical garden round a sunken fountain. He had to abandon it because he did not have enough glass to overwinter the key components of his scheme. When the Exotic Garden replaced the rose garden at Great Dixter, new glass houses and cold frames were soon needed to accommodate the demands of the tender new plants that Fergus and Christopher used in it.

In some gardens the new style coexisted with the old. At Nuneham Park, in 1867, the circular rose garden, with its trellised seats and bowers, was bounded by a ribbon border of subtropicals: scented angel's trumpets (*Brugmansia,* syn. *Datura*) alternating with cannas. Round the outside of that was a wider circle of thorn trees with hollies providing extra shelter and 'completely screening this pretty retired spot', as the *Journal of Horticulture* reported. The screening was important (as at Dixter); it provided physical protection from wind, and a visual shield from the rest of the garden.

Of course, it all meant much more work for the gardeners. Robert Fish wished he could have every pair of hands multiplied threefold. 'Few people know before they try,' he grumbled, 'what it is to fill large flower gardens in the present fashion.' In early spring thousands of pots had to be watered. Later, tender plants had to be successfully hardened off. You needed the right kind of weather for that — calm, with no frost or chilly east wind. The plants had to be moved out as quickly as possible in the morning, when there was the least difference between the inside temperature and the outside. In autumn, dahlias, gladioli and cannas all had to be lifted and stored in frost-free sheds. Dracaenas and other foliage plants and specimen fuchsias were potted and brought under cover. Coleus plants had to be housed to give spring cuttings (the only way to perpetuate the forms with the best foliage). Seed had to collected from the best lobelias and carefully sown in a cold frame.

Not everyone approved of the new subtropical style. If the garden was to be converted into a 'kale-yard, or a place for the vulgar exhibition of meaningless masses of coarse foliage plants, subtropical or otherwise,' spluttered a correspondent in the *Gardeners' Chronicle*, 'then let us boldly call it a leaf garden at once, and at least find a place somewhere for our lovely flowers to exhibit their beauty by themselves.'

Henry Cooke, recreating his dreams of India in the Forest of Dean, was one of the last people to garden wholeheartedly in the exotic style. In 1877, cannas, ginger (*Hedychium*), rice-paper plant (*Tetrapanax*), angel's trumpets and the Abyssinian banana flourished in his Gloucestershire valley, along with the Norfolk Island tree fern (*Cyathea brownii*), grevillea and sparrmannia.

THE FASHION FOR EXOTICS

By the end of the 19th century, the fashion for exotic planting was on the way out. Then when the Great War came there were no men left to stoke the boilers, fumigate glasshouses, haul tender exotics in and out of shelter. After the war, labour was scarce and fuel cost more, too. Though the subtropical style lived on in park bedding schemes of abutilon, canna, coleus, cordyline, eucalyptus, nicotiana, perilla and castor oil plants, the English garden settled into a generally cosy mix of rose beds and herbaceous borders. Rockeries flourished. Dwarf conifers had their day. So did hostas and heathers.

Then, in 1988, a young enthusiast for the exotic, Myles Challis, published his first book, *Exotic Gardening in Cool Climes*. Shortly afterwards, in 1990, Angus White opened his extraordinary nursery, Architectural Plants near Horsham in Sussex, with palms and cycads and spiky exotics to the fore. And then, in 1993, when Christopher threw the roses out of his rose garden at Great Dixter, it was as if someone had chucked the apes off the Rock of Gibraltar. There were full-page spreads in the national press on his bananas and cannas. You expected questions to be raised in the House. In horticultural societies throughout the land, members debated whether this was the end of the world as they knew it. And he, of course, conducting the subtropical orchestra in shirts and knitted waistcoats as outrageously coloured as his cannas, adored the fracas. He always loved to shock.

HARDY and STRUCTURAL ingredients

While they may be perfectly hardy, there are many plants which, either by their intrinsic nature or because of the way we treat them, give an exotic feel.

These are the plants we can risk leaving *in situ* year-round, with just a little or no protection, and yet they will give an impression, during their growing season, of belonging out there in some way. It's a matter of lushness and exuberance, with just that touch of glamour that we do not associate with the cosy normality of a British countryside, charming though that is in its way.

ENFORCED YOUTH

Many vigorous woody plants need particular treatment to create the effect we are after, always remembering our season of interest—from July through to October.

Take *Acer negundo* 'Flamingo'. This is a pink-variegated form of the American box elder, a vigorous but fairly boring tree with pinnate leaves. The variegation is radiant on the leaves' first unfurling but soon settles down to humdrum nonentity, the pink disappearing on mature leaves. But summer-long youth can be imposed by cutting it hard back to a compact framework each spring. This will force it to exploit its natural vigour by making continuous new growth right through to late summer. An extension of young shoots will carry on for three or four months. The young growing tips, which are what you mainly see, have the pink flamingo colouring in all its freshness. We keep what would, untreated, become a tree, down to a managed 4m/13ft bush. The young growth, when bare in winter, is covered with an attractive pale grey bloom. Only in early spring is it all pruned back again, removing weak growth entirely and shortening back the strong to 2.5cm/1in long stumps.

The most attractive feature in many hardy eucalyptus is the juvenile

◀ *The Asian rice-paper plant, Tetrapanax papyrifer, with large, indented palmate leaves, turns us weak at the knees. Young leaves, covered with a thick fawn felt, are particularly attractive. It is amazingly hardy. We lift it in the autumn but the roots left behind start a new colony the following year. The height of this shrub varies according to whether it brings its old wood through the winter or not.*

▲ We impose summer-long youth on *Acer negundo* 'Flamingo', a pink-variegated form of the American box elder, by cutting it hard back to a compact framework each spring (top). *This stimulates it into making new young growth through most of the summer* (above), *instead of having just one spring burst. At the same time, we are keeping it to a manageable size.*

foliage, which is entirely different from the long, thin, drooping leaves on mature trees. Best known of these gums is *Eucalyptus gunnii*, which may grow to 2m/6½ft before the leaf change. But juvenility can be renewed by a hard annual cut-back. In the Exotic Garden, we find it best to replace our plants completely every three years or so and to this end we sow and bring on a fresh batch of seedlings pretty well annually and start selecting early. The seedlings vary a lot in colour; we keep the bluest of them and discard the rest.

Although the juvenile leaves of *Eucalyptus gunnii* clasp the stem to an extent, this feature is far more pronounced in *E. perriniana*, where their stem-clasping forms a perfect circle and the colouring is generally as blue as you could wish. Hardiness is more dodgy, but we can usually hold on to a plant for quite a few years, giving it the usual spring cutting-back treatment.

The juvenile eucalypts are a marvellous foil to neighbouring plants. For instance to the purple colouring and large leaves of the castor bean, *Ricinus communis* 'Carmencita'. Also to bright yellow or red dahlias. Fergus makes use of their framework as a hoist for his pet annual climber *Ipomoea* (*Mina*) *lobata*. We are always aiming at close integration of all our material.

The golden *Catalpa bignonioides* 'Aurea' will make a tree if required, but is far more effective pruned annually to a framework, say 1.5m/5ft high, to encourage large, luminous leaves at a height where you can appreciate them, especially if they have a dark background. All plants have to be grafted and the Dutch make a speciality of this but, unsurprisingly, they cost a lot.

MANIPULATED TREES

I will deal next with two heavily manipulated hardy trees that become unrecognizably exotic if cut annually back to a stump several centimetres or a few inches above ground level. Of the shoots that then sprout from the stump, we allow only one to develop, the others being rubbed out immediately on appearance. Both trees can easily be raised from seed or from root cuttings. As the cutting-back technique weakens the plants after a number of years, they are replaced when signs of this become evident.

Ailanthus altissima, the tree of heaven, is widely grown as a street tree in big, grimy cities. It falls into the 'useful' category; that is serviceable but unexciting and largely taken for granted. I should in fairness add, however, that where summers are warm enough it makes huge bunches of 'keys', which are its developing seeds, and that they are in bright, highly conspicuous shades of pink. Its suckering habit becomes more pronounced if its roots are damaged, in which case new shoots are made from the damaged surfaces. Given the stooling treatment, a plant's appearance is transformed. It makes pinnate leaves 1.5m/5ft long on annual stems growing 4–4.2m/13–14ft tall. Generous feeding helps.

My other example of a tree that we transform with stooling is *Paulownia tomentosa*, a member of the foxglove family, *Scrophulariaceae*, bearing clusters of purple flowers in spring, before the leaves appear. Where the summer

We first establish a young plant of Paulownia tomentosa *and then, after two or three years, cut it almost to the ground each winter, allowing only one or two of the resulting shoots to develop* (left). *We remove any young side shoots at the end of June* (centre). *By August* (right), *with generous feeding, it will be up to 4.2m/14ft tall, bearing only a few leaves, but these are huge, wide and furry.*

▼ *Fergus trims away the suckers beneath the tree of heaven,* Ailanthus altissima (left), *which have been transformed by the stooling treatment. Each season it grows up to 4.2m/14ft tall, with long pinnate leaves, each perhaps 80cm/32in long, though we aim, by generous feeding, to get them longer than that.*

climate is warmer than ours and more ripening, it makes a tremendous show at this stage and I have particularly admired it in Pennsylvania, in the USA, where it self-sows freely. I tried it as a tree myself, at the back of my Long Border, but the flowers never made a great impression and their purple colouring seemed to melt into the sulky background darkness of April-shower-type clouds. As an annually stooled foliage plant it is transformed, with huge, wide furry leaves, a metre or several feet across. They invariably catch the public's attention as there's nothing like them. Remembering that there will be considerable shade beneath them when in full leaf, they can be underplanted with shade lovers and tolerants, like a whole range of begonias or impatiens.

STRUCTURAL SHRUBS

The sumacs are hardy suckering shrubs. *Rhus glabra* 'Laciniata' is no exception and gets all over the place. However, if you have a principal woody crown and prune it annually hard back, it will (until it gets tired of the treatment)

▲ *On a salient corner in the Exotic Garden,* Melianthus major *vies for space with a* Tetrapanax papyrifer *sucker.*

▼ *The young, lush green foliage of honey spurge,* Euphorbia mellifera.

make large and imposing bipinnate leaves of exotic appearance. I should mention that the widely current name that I have used is incorrect and should be *Rhus × pulvinata* Autumn Lace Group.

Melianthus major is my favourite structural foliage plant—when I'm looking at it, anyway. Its hardiness can be doubtful and a bit of trouble may need taking, but the fact that my oldest and most handsome colony has been established for some fifty years speaks for itself. Moreover it came to me from John Treasure's garden in the frosty Teme Valley of the West Midlands and he kept it going successfully. It is a woody plant but apt to lose its top growth in winter frost. Had this survived the winter, it would have flowered the following year but the flowers are insignificant and it is no loss to forego them. Furthermore, plants that retain their old wood become gawky and generally unattractive. Freshest and most comely growth pushes through from below ground level.

I need to repeat what I have written elsewhere about *Melianthus major*. Old stems are left through the winter as they provide anchorage for a thick layer of fern fronds, put in position after the first killer frost, generally in December. In spring, this blanket is removed ahead of new shoots making their appearance. If you want to propagate from a good stock plant, having all the best attributes, these shoots are the best to use. You won't get many of them but quality is assured, whereas seedlings, although temptingly easy to raise, often give rise to inferior stock, with smaller leaves lacking substance. This has, in fact, been my experience on a salient corner in my Exotic Garden. Currently the situation seems to have been rescued through a *Tetrapanax papyrifer* sucker, with its bold, broad, undivided leaf, arising bang in the middle of the melianthus.

M. major has glaucous pinnate leaves with jagged margins. The pinnae are somewhat incurved and their margins cast alluring shadows, one against another, especially noticeable when the sun is low and shadows long. From being cut back in spring, growth is slow to get going but it becomes increasingly imposing right through to late autumn, when that killer frost comes along. A rich red dahlia, such as 'Grenadier', looks especially telling in conjunction with the glaucous foliage of melianthus.

Also tender, but well worth planting in a warm corner, is the evergreen honey spurge, *Euphorbia mellifera* (2.5m/8ft). Young plants are particularly handsome, so I replace mine at frequent intervals. It is the lush green foliage you want—the honey-scented flowers are insignificant and, appearing in spring, too early for our purpose. We prune out a good deal of flowered wood in the summer to make way for young shoots. The Himalayan *E. donii* (which was first distributed as *E. longifolia*), is one of the most striking of all herbaceous spurges, clump forming to 1.5m/5ft and in flower non-stop—smart, lime-green flowers from July to October. It needs support. We give it three or four canes when it is about two thirds grown, twisting a single piece of string around each stout stem and taking it from cane to cane.

Some shrubs that flower too early for our purpose provide structure. *Sophora* 'Little Baby' is a New Zealander that has been hardy in my Exotic Garden for a number of years. It makes a tight little bush (1.2m/4ft) with neat, evergreen pinnate leaves. Its yellow pea flowers, in spring, are tucked away in the centre of the bush and don't make any sort of show. A talking point, let's say. The bush itself, with its tangle of twisted branches, is the attraction.

Acacia pravissima is a wattle that might pass unnoticed at the height of the Exotic Garden's summer season were it not for its small, sharply pointed, triangular leaves. It has vigour and develops into a tall shrub with astonishing speed. From seed, flowering will probably start in its third year and quickly becomes abundant in its February to April season. The whole plant is then plastered with neat, scented yellow pompons. Certainly cause for making a detour into this bit of garden's off-season. As with many acacias, the flower buds are already visible in the previous autumn. To gloat would be dangerous (although hard to avoid), because *A. pravissima*'s hardiness in much of Britain is questionable. Well worth a bash, however. Give it sun and shelter.

BOLD FOLIAR FEATURES

Big lush leaves and strong shapes form the bones of the Exotic Garden and there's no better plant for achieving a tropical effect than the hardy Japanese banana, *Musa basjoo*. Three specimens remain in the Exotic Garden year-round but need help. It has typical banana leaves that shred in high winds but given really warm weather in July, a new leaf will be put out every ten days. A good contrasting companion to grow underneath this banana is the Egyptian papyrus, *Cyperus papyrus*, but that is by no means hardy.

Musas, in contrast to *Ensete*, the other principal genus of bananas, makes multiple stems and new shoots from well below soil level. We dig up the whole lot each spring and sort out what we want to keep. Single stems look best, but which stem? If you choose one that will run up to flower during the summer, the party will be over, as this will bring all growth to an end and there'll be no more fresh young leaves. If the chosen shoot is too young and small, it'll make no significant display in the current year. You must learn to choose a shoot that is large enough to perform significantly but not so large as to flower. All the superfluous shoots can be potted up to make new plants, if you want them.

In late autumn, we wrap the banana stems up, tightly, into a dense bolster of fern, including bracken, fronds. In a mild winter, new green growth will often poke out at the top of the bolster. It'll probably get frosted but take no notice. Just wait till May before unwrapping and sorting things out as I have described.

There are a good many more *Musa* cultivars available, mainly derived from *M. acuminata*, so it's worth keeping your eyes open. Our friend, Dennis Schrader, of Landcraft Environments in Mattituck, NY, has written to Fergus

▲ *Light and shadows on* Musa basjoo.

▼ *The Chusan or Chinese windmill palm,* Trachycarpus fortunei, *needs the shelter of a warm wall to protect it from winds that can scorch its huge, fan-shaped leaves.*

◄◄ In a sheltered position and during the warmest weather, Musa basjoo produces a new, 2m/6½ft-long leaf every week or ten days. As plants grow and expand, upwards and sideways, the atmosphere in the Exotic Garden becomes more intimate. After rain, when the plants flop over the paths even more, wet legs or ankles are a fair price to pay for the sensation of swishing through the jungle. The choice of material next to paths needs careful consideration. Colocasia foliage may be dripping but is otherwise kind to swishers-by, whereas Yucca gloriosa, seen here with the 1.5m/5ft panicle of creamy bells it suddenly produces in September, must be set well back, since its stiff and sharply pointed leaves are a threat to passers-by.

◄ Astelia chathamica has soft, grey- and silver-green sword leaves that twist to reveal the pale undersides. They catch the light at varying angles and look strong without the stiffness or solemnity of, say, Yucca gloriosa. It is none too hardy but— dare we say it?—so far so good.

▼ Yucca flaccida is smaller than Y. gloriosa and, as the common name— weakleaf yucca—suggests, of softer texture, the leaves being limp. We have planted the cultivar 'Ivory' by the path in Bed 1 (see the plan on pages 18–19). The flowers are earlier (July with us) and borne in broad panicles, waxy, white and bell-shaped.

recommending *Musa sikkimensis*, *M. itinerans* and *M. lasiocarpa*: 'They make majestic plants providing coarse texture in heights ranging from 1–5m/ 3–16½ft.' I discuss a tender beauty in another chapter.

Yucca is a large American genus, many of whose members are tender in Britain. Or else, having grown for a number of years, they flower and subsequently die. At the end of May, you will see *Y. whipplei* flowering dramatically on the steep, otherwise entirely grassy hills around Los Angeles, the grass itself being generally burnt up and brown by then. Although this yucca generally dies after flowering, there are strains of it in which the main flowering crown dies but there are vegetative pups around it to carry a colony through to future years. Best of these and altogether a handsomer plant is subspecies *parishii*. The height of *Y. whipplei* at flowering is variable, depending largely on residual moisture left over from the February rainy season. It is likely to be 4.5 to 6m/15ft to 20ft.

The familiar *Yucca gloriosa* makes a dome of stiff, spine-tipped, solemn green leaves and is generally described as an architectural plant, drawing attention to itself in any crowd. After flowering, which is not to be missed, the flowered crown divides into several smaller crowns. An old specimen becomes woody, and attains a height of 2m/6½ft or more—a community of variously sized crowns. 'Variegata', in which the leaves are boldly striped yellow, is slightly less vigorous but otherwise similar and as ready to flower and subsequently branch.

There are several other worthwhile garden species, such as *Yucca recurvifolia*, having a similar habit to *Y. gloriosa* but with softer leaves that bend back on themselves. *Y. flaccida* has an especially free-flowering clone, 'Ivory'. It is stemless, all the crowns arising from ground level and to a height of 1.2m/4ft or so. You saw out flowered crowns and others take their place. *Y. filamentosa* is a pretty, freely flowering, low-growing species, especially charming in yellow-variegated 'Variegata'. A good focal point on a promontory in a small-scale setting.

A luxuriant deciduous plant that makes 1.8 to 2.4m/6 to 8ft of growth in a season is *Polymnia sonchifolia*, called yacon when its tubers are used as food. It is good for diabetics, being sweet but without starch or sugar. The big leaves are more or less triangular, slightly rough-textured, flabby, more than 30cm/1ft across. It is a bold foliar feature. The flowers are common-looking little yellow daisies, but they're not produced outdoors in our climate.

There are two species of southern hemisphere *Astelia* easily grown in warmer gardens of southern Britain. In rather key positions, where they are free to draw attention to themselves, I have several plants of *A. chathamica*, from the Chatham Islands. It isn't in the Exotic Garden, but for no particular reason. Its bold, yet pliable sword leaves are in several shades of silver and grey, both the top and the undersides showing. This makes a lively impression on a plant 1.2m/4ft high. In one key position at the top of the Long Border, it shows up importantly from 137m/150 yards. I am keen to get it a mate as with

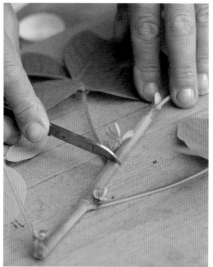

We can never have enough Amicia zygomeris (above left). It is probably hardy enough with us to come through the winter and we are experimenting by leaving it in situ with bark mounded over it. But we play safe by taking plenty of semi-ripe cuttings in October/November. We have everything ready, including 9cm/3in pots filled with 50:50 damp cutting compost and grit. Kathleen Leighton (above right) says she tries to allow as short an interval as possible to elapse between removing cuttings from a bush and preparing them. This is the procedure:

• Cut a terminal shoot without flowers just below a leaf node (joint), dropping them into a dry plastic bag and closing it at the neck.
• Use a sharp knife to trim the cuttings to length (5–10cm/2–4in long). If you are interrupted, put the cuttings back into the plastic bag to keep them plump. Never let them wilt.

• While the cutting is still damp, dip it in hormone rooting compound (this must be fresh or it is counterproductive) and tap off excess powder on the edge of the lid.
• Insert the cuttings, firming in with your fingertips. Cover with a loosely knotted polythene bag, secured with a rubber band, or place in an unventilated cold frame, out of full sun. Keep the cuttings moist, that is neither dry nor saturated. Pot on when shoots have sprouted.

cross-pollination it is capable of producing brilliant crops of red berries. I have been given seed and now have a good batch of seedlings. We shall see, but a hard winter could knock it back. Fingers crossed.

A. nervosa 'Westland' (from the wet Westland district in New Zealand) has narrow leaves with a metallic sheen. Their colouring is complex, in bronzy grey and warm brown. This is a newcomer to the Exotic Garden. One is experimenting non-stop.

Amicia zygomeris magnetizes our attention. We can't quite make it out. Officially a shrub we need, in the garden, to treat it as a herbaceous foliage plant, seldom producing its yellow pea flowers, although these are abundant, late summer, in warmer countries. This legume was introduced from Mexico in 1826 and was named after an Italian physician, Amici, of that period. From ground level, it annually makes 2.5m/8ft-tall shoots clothed in pinnate foliage, each leaf with two opposite leaflets. These are roughly triangular, with a broad distal base. It is broadly notched — a dip rather than a V. They certainly look unusual. In the evening, sleep movements are very pronounced, the entire leaf in a state of semi-collapse.

We have two kinds of New Zealand flax in the Exotic Garden — more for their fans of evergreen strap leaves than for the flowering stems that have generally gone over by high summer. *Phormium cookianum* subsp. *hookeri* 'Tricolor' (1.2m/4ft) has arching leaves that are green in the centre, then striped green and pale yellow and purplish red along the margins. It is reliably hardy here. *P.* 'Sundowner' (1.8m/6ft) has a more upright habit, the leaves alternating pink with dusky green. A tidying up at winter's end involves cutting out the dead leaves, which can be quite time-consuming. Phormium clumps expand in bulk over the years and eventually need dividing.

▼ Phormium cookianum *subsp.* hookeri *'Tricolor' has arching leaves that are green in the centre, then striped green and pale yellow and purplish red along the margins. It remains smart throughout the year and is reliably hardy with us. Flowering spikes are an interesting and beautiful event in early summer, arising like cranes' necks and bills, and numerous enough to make a strong and exotic impression. The pendent seed pods are spirally twisted.*

▼▶ *The pink and dusky green leaves of* Phormium *'Sundowner' make a spiky backdrop to dazzling dahlias as well as a degree of shade for the intricately patterned foliage of begonias, including* B. luxurians *with leaves divided into long fingers and 'Little Brother Montgomery' with jagged, pointed foliage.*

▲ Miscanthus sinensis 'Variegatus' makes a graceful foliage feature, rising like a fountain above the plantings around it. The leaves striped in green and white are a good foil for a rose that continues to earn its keep—Rosa 'Madge', blush-pink and smelling of R. arvensis.

Ornamental grasses with lush foliage have their place but should be kept in it, and that involves care and attention. Well treated and watered, *Miscanthus sinensis* 'Variegatus' (2m/6½ft when established), makes a graceful foliage feature in the Exotic Garden, rising like a fountain above the plantings around it. The leaves striped in green and white are exciting seen against the dark yew hedge behind and the variegation strengthens as the season progresses. What I'd call a class act. The miscanthus are clump forming and fall off in quality eventually. They need to be dug up and replanted in improved soil, but will sulk for the first year afterwards.

In a garden setting, the giant reed grass, *Arundo donax,* makes a bold feature and, in our British climate, it does not get out of hand, as it has in swampy areas of California, where its blocking of waterways is a considerable menace. In the marshy Camargue, in southern France, it is planted along dyke margins as a windbreak. As it is never pruned in any way, it looks pretty hideous. In a garden, you routinely cut old stems right to the ground when they start to look tatty in late winter. I find its height (3.6m/12ft) and glaucous colouring an excellent foil in a large bed of hummocky hydrangeas. It is also a focal feature in a raised position in my Exotic Garden. This needs regular, heavy watering if the reed's lower leaves are not to die prematurely, in summer. Its variegated variety is choice and choosy (don't be put off) and features in another chapter.

Bamboos are the most exciting of all grasses but I never seem to have enough spaces to fit them in appropriately. There are bamboos and bamboos and I am not here concerned with the widely ground-covering kinds that will take your garden over completely if given the chance. The really useful and stylish ones are clump-forming. I must add that how they behave depends very much on climate and moisture availability. If we accept that there is a greenhouse effect, it follows that bamboos that were perfectly behaved and predictable, now run about in an unpredictable fashion which may take us completely by surprise. After the hot summer of 2003, previously well-behaved bamboos that kept themselves to themselves made long rhizomes a little below the soil surface, which then popped up, in 2004, a considerable distance from the parent colony. All this depends very much on the climate where you live, so there are no hard and fast rules. You must experiment.

Botanists are forever messing around with the naming and classification of bamboos and they do not agree among themselves but it has been generally agreed to break up the genus *Arundinaria*, of which few now remain. Two of the commonest, *A. murielae* and *A. nitida*, are now both *Fargesia*. They make dense thickets and are good on boundaries instead of a hedge but do need containing.

The joker in the pack is *Chusquea culeou*, from Chile and Argentina, which I grow as a solo feature on my front lawn. It is a tremendously variable species, sometimes tall, sometimes half height. We all discovered just how variable, in a great many ways, when all the chusqueas belonging to the same clone, which was most of those up and down the country, flowered the same year. Hitherto, we had been propagating vegetatively from offsets. This was quite laborious and chusqueas were expensive. But after flowering, there was a great setting of viable seed, which germinated like mustard and cress and the price of chusqueas plummeted. This intermittent flowering of bamboos is quite a feature of them, occurring at widely varying intervals.

Chusquea culeou has solid culms, not hollow as in most bamboos, and the distance between nodes is very short. There is a big tuft of foliage, almost completely surrounding each node, creating a brush-like effect. A clump increases steadily in circumference and is hard work to reduce, with a saw or axe, cutting or chopping under the soil surface. Very hard on the axe blade.

Unpruned bamboos become dense and middle-age looking. Most are greatly improved by annual pruning. The object is to thin out all the weakest and the oldest culms, cutting them right down to ground level, leaving no snags. Not only does this rejuvenate the colony, but it enables you to see through the remaining culms and to what lies beyond them. It has a lightening effect.

Semiarundinaria fastuosa has style, being tall and stately (*fastuosa* means stately). Its upright habit ensures that it doesn't flop over its neighbours. It makes an imposing solo feature. In rich soil (which ours has), it is quite wicked at the root and an effort to control.

The habit of the vast-leaved, South American *Gunnera manicata*, as with many rhizomatous plants, is to move ever outwards, leaving the colony's centre bare. Into this, by the side of our horse pond, I planted the bamboo *Thamnocalamus tessellatus* as a complete contrast. It is the only bamboo from South Africa where, however, it covers enormous areas. It makes grey-green brushes of exuberant foliage. The two plants together are splendidly exotic.

Phyllostachys as a genus seems to me more open-textured and to have greater style than the rest. One side of the culm is flat, the other rounded, the flat and the rounded alternating between nodes. *P. nigra* is immensely variable. Its specific epithet refers to its black culms and they are what one hopes for, the blacker the more distinguished looking. Often they're not. You really need to search around, not necessarily alighting on a named clone.

One of the best known and most widely offered is 'Boryana'; I can't see why. I have a great lump of it—oh yes; it does get regularly pruned and thinned. But it doesn't give me any special pleasure. The culms are messily blotched. So they are in f. *punctata*, but in this case mine has the advantage of spraying outwards from a narrow base. It contrasts well with the *Buddleja* 'Dartmoor' behind it and has sprays of *Clematis* × *jouiniana* 'Praecox' investigating it. A pleasant team. My uniformly blackest clone, black from the first year, came to me without a name. As pruning usually consists of removing all culms, in spring, older than the previous year's, you need these to assume their blackness immediately, not after a year or two.

▼ *Arundo donax is the tallest, noblest grass we can enjoy in our neck of the woods, and its domineering presence is especially striking on mornings when a mist drifts in from the sea. This giant reed grass makes a fine, rather bamboo-like, central feature in the Exotic Garden, rising to 3.6m/12ft or so from nothing, with glaucous foliage arranged in two ranks, arching to the horizontal at their tips.*

◀ Dicksonia squarrosa *is a very exotic-looking New Zealander, the fronds forming a small umbrella on top of the trunk. It is quite a challenge—needing a sheltered position where sun and wind won't burn the foliage, constant moisture in the summer months and protection in winter. Neither trunk nor roots should be allowed to dry out; the more moisture you give it, the better it will thrive. In the wild, the dead fronds cling to the trunk, forming a skirt, to prevent it from losing moisture. The orbicular, glossy leaves of* Farfugium japonicum, *up to 15cm/6in across, give complete contrast of shape and texture.*

▼ *The tassel fern,* Polystichum polyblepharum, *is an excellent shade plant. To see the fronds rising snakily from a circle of scaly, brown bumps is a good reason for making a spring detour to the Exotic Garden when not much else is happening. 'What are you up to, down there?' you ask of them, because they have a curiously animal-like quality. By midsummer they are background players, the deep green fronds adding substance to begonia plantings in Bed 4 (see page 48).*

DESIRABLE FERNS

A desirable 'tree' fern, *Dicksonia squarrosa*, deserves special treatment *in situ*. It does warrant tree fern status as it has a short, stocky trunk. So far I've been able to protect mine in winter with a wooden-framed plastic cover, the fern's crown being packed around with bracken fronds. When it gets taller I shall have to give it the *Musa basjoo* treatment but I hope that some of its live fronds can be overwintered unfrosted, as that will give it a head start in the next growing season and the new crop of fronds will be that much the stronger. It is bipinnate, each frond a handsome entity. There is a most satisfying hard-textured feel to it, when you grasp one. The fact that it is dwarf means that you can look down into its crown, which is itself satisfying.

There are many good hardy ferns to our purpose. My original plant of *Polystichum polyblepharum* was given me by Alan Leslie and from that Fergus has raised it from spores, so we have quite a lot, now. It is evergreen, not more than 30cm/1ft tall and the bipinnate fronds, which have a curve to them, are glossy, rich green. Excellent in a colony where there's a good deal of shade.

Also needing a good bit of shade, and more moisture than most, is *Dryopteris erythrosora* (60cm/2ft), from Japan. New fronds, in shades between orange-red and warm brown that gradually turn green, are produced throughout the summer.

▲ Blechnum fluvatile, *with narrow fronds forming a rosette, is good for shade since it comes from damp areas of forest throughout New Zealand.*

▶ *Some of the roses that still earn their keep in the Exotic Garden: 'Florence Mary Morse' (top), 'White Wings' (centre) and 'Ballerina' (bottom).*

▼ *The soft shield fern has many variations,* Polystichum setiferum *Cristatum Group having lightly crested pinnules and frond tips.*

Blechnum penna-marina from New Zealand is a nice example of the hard ferns, once-pinnate with neat, rounded pinnae on a compact, 30cm/1ft-tall plant. Those are the sterile fronds, the fertile ones clustered in the centre of a plant and rising vertically. They give the plant its height.

Pteris cretica is a popular windowsill plant but surprisingly hardy in some strains. It seeds itself enthusiastically in cold greenhouses, especially under the benches. When such houses have tumbled down, through old age and neglect, the ribbon ferns (often variegated) will survive in the open perfectly happily. The fronds are characteristic, with pinnae in pairs, two, four or six, and a long terminal pinna.

The choice of ferns is limitless and many look suitable in the Exotic Garden where there is shade and they can combine with broad-leaved plants. One old-stager is our native soft shield fern, *Polystichum setiferum*. My elder brother, Oliver, was a keen caver in the Mendip hills. He used to map caves, especially in County Clare, west Ireland. He noticed the ferns growing at the entrance to these caves and brought the polystichum back for me. (It actually grows wild in a wood a quarter mile from Dixter, but his was special and it still flourishes many years after his death.)

HARDY FOLIAGE PLANTS

A *Hosta* well worth including in the Exotic Garden is 'Sum and Substance'. It has outstandingly large leaves of a yellowish green and they are so thick that slugs and snails cannot penetrate them, only nibble away the surface and that is hardly noticeable.

Common and widespread though it is, *Fatsia japonica* must not be forgotten. Large fingered leaves on a shrub that will grow 3m/10ft high and a good deal wider. These leaves are leathery and evergreen. In late autumn, it surprises by producing panicles of white ivy-like blossom. It belongs to the ivy family, *Araliaceae* and the hybrid between it and ivy, × *Fatshedera lizei* is wonderful for a shady position, where its glossy leaves reflect all the light that's going.

Desmodium yunnanense (syn. *D. praestans*), is a legume with miserable little pea flowers if you let it reach that stage. Grow it as a foliage plant, cutting it hard back annually in spring to a 1.2m/4ft framework. It will then produce long wands of glamorous foliage. Unusual in a legume, whose leaves are most often pinnate, these are simple and almost round—a row of them presenting themselves at eye height so that you can't miss them.

Aralias belong to the ivy family and most are woody. The habit of *Aralia elata* is sturdy and uncompromising. It makes upright sticks from ground level to 4.5m/15ft or so, these stems covered in thorns. Of a suckering habit, a grove is most impressive, especially if you can look down a bank on to the top of it because its crown explodes, in autumn, into a mass of tiny white blossom. The leaves assume autumnal tints. There are two choice, that is extremely expensive, variegated forms, white in 'Variegata' and yellow in

'Aureovariegata', with large pinnate leaves on a shrub of moderate height. Watch out for green-leaved suckers. These are most likely to be produced if the roots are damaged.

Two beautiful herbaceous species are available, with bold pinnate leaves. They can be fine lawn specimens. Their height varies from 1.8 to 4.5m/6ft to 15ft. *A. cachemirica* comes from one side of the world; *A. californica* from the other. They make big panicles of purple, ivy-like flowers which then fruit handsomely, with purple berries and supporting stalks.

Hydrangea aspera subsp. *sargentiana* has large furry leaves, especially imposing when grown in shade, which it anyway requires to prevent it scorching. The pale mauve, lacecap flowers are suitable adjuncts.

Rubus lineatus, of the bramble family, can be treated in either of two ways. Pruned to the ground annually, the resulting foliage, borne on wands 60cm/2ft high, are a feast in themselves. They are elliptical, undivided with toothed margins, green on top but silvery underneath. Or you can let it go for two years, in which case, being of a suckering habit, it makes a 1.8m/6ft-high thicket, bearing blackberry-like fruit. Fergus likes it that way but I think the hard-pruned plant looks more exotic.

RELIABLE COLOUR

Shapes are everything but colour is also important in plants that stay put year round. They must be strong enough to cope with the hurly-burly of the Exotic Garden. They also need to perform at the right time of year and for as long a season as possible. Agapanthus flowers come and go much too quickly to earn a place, and *Arum creticum* bears its dramatic yellow spathes for a few days in April—obviously far too early for our purpose.

There are still about ten vigorous rose bushes left (and there are still visitors who make a beeline for one or other of these and pretend that nothing else grows here). Among them are several bushes of 'Madge'— blush-pink and smelling of *R. arvensis*—which continue to earn their keep. And 'Mrs Oakley Fisher', with single apricot flowers, which was given to me as a cutting from Sissinghurst by Vita Sackville-West.

Impatiens tinctoria is at its peak in summer and autumn, which is just what we are after. It may not be trustworthy—it is easy enough to safeguard your stock by rooting cuttings under frost-free glass—but will often, given a bit of help, come through the winter outside. We cover its crown with a thick layer of fern fronds. Removed in spring, the impatiens will soon sprout and will grow 2.5m/8ft tall in the course of the summer. Don't place it in a prominent position; its foliage is hideously coarse, albeit soft and flabby. The point of it is the wide-open, sizeable flowers, which are white but with a bold purple centre. They are heavily, exotically night-scented. As the plant makes wide clumps, we chop a large portion of it off each spring. One plant is plenty.

Against the roof of the hovel, nearby, we grow *Escallonia bifida* (it is one parent of the better known 'Iveyi'). We do have another plant in a more open position, so it's not too desperately tender. A run of kind winters is rather important. The shrub itself is hardly an object of beauty and needs tidying up each spring, by removing last year's old flowering remnants. Its flowering is latish—August–September, and it is then smothered in domed panicles of white, star-shaped blossom. It stops you in your tracks, especially when, as in most years, it is covered in butterflies. It is especially beloved of Painted Ladies and Red Admirals, whose numbers, however, fluctuate widely from year to year as they are migrants and go through many hazards. Comma and Tortoiseshell butterflies are other keen visitors. Just now and again, you see hardly any butterflies at all, but this is almost certainly because there are hardly any of them about. Bees and other insects are equally keen—you are watching a huge community.

In the tropics, where it is too warm for clematis, they make do with thunbergias. It is lucky for us that clematis, many of which come in exotic colours, proportions and profusion, are completely at home in our climate. The hybrids that get into their flowering stride after the middle of June give us a succession of reliable colour. The pruning of late-flowering clematis is straightforward—any time between November and April we reduce all the previous season's shoots to within a pair of buds at the base, leaving a woody stump about 60cm/2ft high. One of my oldest plants is 'Marcel Moser', a large-flowered hybrid which grows up a post supporting the hovel roof. Obviously of the same vintage as Nelly, it is rosy mauve with a deep carmine bar but has longer sepals and is better in the sun. The next to flower, in July, is 'Madame Julia Correvon' whose small wine-red flowers with cream centres give us cascades of colour on a 4m/13ft chestnut pole. The other clematis in the Exotic Garden is 'Victoria', a favourite with me because its flowers are

large (12–20cm/5–8in) and an attractive, not too heavy shade of purple.

Some kniphofias, the red-hot pokers, flower too early and where their long, stringy evergreen leaves are in evidence, can be something of a liability. There are two exceptions that I make use of, even though on the edge of paving, where the lankiness of leaves is most in evidence.

Kniphofia linearifolia has, I understand, a widespread distribution in its native South Africa, which will make it a variable species. In my clone, the leaves are bright green and therefore, I consider, an asset *per se*. Most green foliage goes heavy as summer progresses but not in this case. The typically orange pokers come almost as a surprise, in October — a great sheaf of them. In another part of my garden they look particularly splendid in front of the white pampas plumes of *Cortaderia selloana* 'Pumila'. I do not include any pampas in the Exotic Garden, as it is far from companionable, its sharp-edged, spreading leaves keeping at bay anything in the nature of a close neighbour.

Kniphofia caulescens is my other poker. As its name suggests, it has woody stems. To prevent it from gangling, we replant pretty frequently. The leaves are glaucous. Its orange pokers appear, all in a rush, in September. That's the normal strain, but another that I had from Helen Dillon flowers in June. It is stingy with propagation material, though I find it the handsomer of the two.

There is a nasty bacterial disease which can polish kniphofias off in double quick time. Watch out for sudden, unexplained death and lose no time in throwing out the victims, together with the soil around them. Don't replant with pokers there for a while.

Fuchsias are legion but their foliage is generally a great let-down. That is what, for me, spoils exhibits of fuchsias at flower shows, however abundant their blossom. Of course I have to grow some — the dwarf 'Alice Hoffman', for instance in red and white (double). The double 'Lena' is another, blush white with a fully double centre. It starts flowering in late June and just carries on. About 30cm/1ft tall with stems that arch under the weight of the blossom.

Just a few fuchsias are worth growing for their foliage, in its own right. 'Mr West' is one such, a confection of pink and cream being concentrated in the margin and mid-rib. Its habit is prostrate, making it suitable for hanging baskets, of which I have none, so I grow it horizontally on a paved corner in the Exotic Garden.

Cuphea cyanea comes through some winters. When that happens it gets a head start, like a good many other plants we've been discussing. It has racemes of tubular flowers. The base and main length of the tube is orange. This grades to yellow and the mouth (it is a Mexican cigar plant) is lime green. Quite a colour range but in a demure plant, up to 60cm/2ft tall in its second year and all the better and taller if it gets a hoist from a close neighbour. I also use it in ornamental pots where it contrasts pleasingly with the blue daisies of *Felicia amelloides*.

▲ Kniphofia linearifolia *is a handsome poker with foliage that earns its keep by being bright green. The pokers really are red hot, coming in October in one glorious rush, and look very handsome with the dark leaves of castor oil and* Dahlia *'David Howard'.*

▶ Cuphea cyanea *is a small, tender shrub from Mexico with quite a colour range: the orange tubular flowers grade to yellow and the mouth is lime green. If it comes through the winter, it reaches 60cm/2ft in its second year, and flowers to mid-September. We also use it in pot displays.*

▼ Fuchsia *'Mr West' is low growing and one of the best variegated cultivars.*

Begonia grandis subsp. evansiana *is the only hardy begonia we grow, seen here in Bed 4 with the fern,* Polystichum polyblepharum. *The begonia's large, ovate, olive-green leaves have red-tinted undersides and attractive red veining.*

▼ *Above iris-like leaves* Tigridia pavonia, *from Mexico, makes a succession of blooms in an amazing colour range through much of the summer, although each lasts only for a day.*

▼▼ *The ginger lilies are herbaceous perennials with thick rhizomes.* Hedychium densiflorum 'Assam Orange' *flowers for several months, each salmon-orange spike often followed by chains of orange, berry-like fruits. They are reputedly fragrant.*

TUBERS, CORMS AND RHIZOMES

Of the many begonias I grow, *Begonia grandis* subsp. *evansiana* (60cm/2ft) is the only one that is hardy. (I deal with the tenders later.) It is a nice soft shade of pink. I wouldn't mind its being late-flowering if it didn't suddenly drop all its blossom before there's a sniff of frost. There is also a white version, which I don't rate highly, but that's just me. The flowers are quite small. Nice but unexciting.

Tigridia pavonia must get a mention. Sometimes its corms survive the winter, especially against a warm wall, sometimes not, but they are so cheaply replaced from the spring bulb catalogues that one doesn't need to worry. They flower only in the morning, their silken gauds (visibly related to irises) opening wide and revealing three limbs, the colour (which varies widely in different strains) plain at the extremities but heavily, improbably spotted in a cupped, central zone. Corms divide rapidly and seed sets freely, so if you're paying attention and don't let the lot get frosted, you need never be without.

Hedychiums belong to the ginger family, *Zingiberaceae*, and they have rhizomatous roots just below the soil surface. The thick fleshy rhizome builds up over the years and there's a visible joint, shown by a dip, between years. Not many are hardy, but *H. densiflorum* (90cm/3ft) seems to be entirely so. It makes a colony and comes very late into growth. This allows me to take advantage of the spring and early summer vacant space, which I do with the pink, April-flowering cranesbill, *Geranium albanum*. By the end of May, this has done its stuff and is ready for long retirement.

In July, the hedychium opens a succession of dense, biscuit-coloured spikes. Each spike may not last much above three days, the individual flowers in it all coming together, but there are plenty of arrows in the quiver, so you get decent value. Kingdon Ward's introduction of the improved 'Assam Orange' grows about 30cm/1ft taller and is a notably deeper, richer orange.

Hedychium densiflorum 'Stephen' (90cm/3ft) is fitted in here. It was, like 'Tara' (see below), introduced from Nepal by Tony Schilling. He named it after his son. The spikes are short and broad, cream-coloured and sweetly night-scented. They, like the others, don't last long and colonies increase fairly slowly. But worth it, definitely.

Hedychium forrestii is a favourite at Dixter. Over a period of months it grows to 1.8m/6ft or more and its foliage is a notably fresh green. A great background for the salmon pink, glaucous-leaved *Canna* 'Erebus', for instance, but you can think of many alternatives.

Hedychium coccineum is rather less hardy than the above and needs a nice hot position. It grows especially well in the cottage garden at Sissinghurst Castle. That is the clone which Tony Schilling introduced from Nepal and named 'Tara', after his daughter. At 1.2m/4ft, it is extremely showy with a broad orange and red (the stamens) raceme. It all flowers together but the display is short-lived.

Roy Lancaster

EXOTICS IN A SUBURBAN GARDEN

Perhaps it is as a result of my upbringing and early Parks training in a northern industrial town that I hanker for anything exotic that offers an escape from the drab, soot-coated shrubberies of my youth.

THE SO-CALLED broad-leaved cabbage tree, *Cordyline indivisa*, from New Zealand is the perfect antidote for any lingering sombre memories, and the fact that I have seen it growing in the wild adds immeasurably to the attraction. It is by far the most exotic plant in my Hampshire garden. Before I go any further, let me say that any large-leaved or strikingly flowered plant that reminds me of travels in warmer climes qualifies, in my garden, as exotic.

It was while visiting the Tongariro National Park in North Island (the Mount Doom location for the film *The Lord of the Rings*) that I first saw this cabbage tree, which is a member of the *Agave* family. They were of variable age and size, from the huge, stemless rosettes of young plants to single-stemmed adults of up to 6m/20ft and more. The sight of these cordylines in the shadow of an active volcano is one of the most dramatic plant-related scenes I have ever encountered, and the single specimen in my suburban garden is a continuing reminder of it.

My plant is now 2m/6½ft tall on a short stem, while the leathery, strap-shaped, gently tapering leaves are over 90cm/3ft long and exquisitely coloured: bloomy green and erect when young, shining green on the spreading older leaves below. The strong midrib is an old gold above and red-tinted on the silvery white under-surface. This plant dominates its immediate

space in the same way that a tree fern would, and is the final, jaw-dropping surprise when visitors, wearied by detail, reach the bottom of the garden. It grows happily enough in my clay soil, sheltered from strong winds, and no longer needs the winter protection it received in its early years.

EXOTIC FLOWERS

For exotic flowers I rely on the cockscomb coral tree, *Erythrina crista-galli*, from South America. In the wild it can make a woody-stemmed shrub to a height of 5m/16½ft or more, while here it survives our less favoured conditions by behaving like a herbaceous perennial. The eager young growths, asparagus-green and succulent, emerge in May or early June. By July they will have reached 1.5m/5ft and be bearing large, long-stalked, thrice-divided leaves. Stems, stalks and leaf-lets beneath are furnished with hooked prickles of varying size that make handling this plant a potentially painful experience. Meanwhile, the stronger shoots are producing bold terminal racemes of up to 60cm/2ft long which bear, at intervals, clusters of seriously large, fleshy, deep scarlet, long-stalked pea flowers; shiny in bud before expanding to reveal a claw-like keel and a broad standard in a cup-like calyx. The effect of six or eight of these inflorescences is stunning.

Some years ago I was given a small but viciously spiny *Puya alpestris*, a member of the pineapple family from the Chilean Andes. I have seen the similar *P. berteroana* on the hills above Santiago, occupying the sun-baked, scrub-clad, stone-scattered slopes in the unlikely, but exciting, company of cacti, alstro-emerias, giant lobelias and wine palms. The huge, dense, greyish rosettes of spine-toothed, curving, sword-shaped leaves stud the landscape. Plants of a certain maturity send forth an erect, stout-stemmed flowering spike up to 2m/6½ft, the upper region sporting short, spiky branches studded with three-petalled waxy flowers of an astonishing deep jade green.

After seeing these wild colonies in flower, the

▶ *The Chusan or Chinese windmill palm,* Trachycarpus fortunei, *is one of the permanent fixtures in Christopher's Exotic Garden, providing a leg-up for evergreen* Escallonia bifida *on its way to the roof of the hovel.*

thought of *Puya alpestris* flowering in my garden filled me with great anticipation. Having grown it in a succession of pots to accommodate its increasing size, I decided it needed a permanent home in the ground, but where would I find a space offering sun, warmth, good drainage and shelter? The answer presented itself when I decided to remove a large *Daphne bholua* from a corner flanking the west wall of the house, directly beneath the canopy above our front door. That was six years ago, since when it has increased in size to an alarming 1.5 by 2m/5 by 6½ft. Encouraged by that progress, I have added three other puyas to that bed, including the yellow-flowered *P. chilensis*.

The one drawback, apart from the fact that they have yet to flower, is that the puyas now block access to the gas meter. Every time the inspector calls I have to use a stout bamboo pole to prise the bristling armature aside. One inspector told me it is worse than facing a snappy dog. Perhaps that is why the same man never calls twice. I was not surprised recently to hear

that, in the wild, puyas are regarded as hazardous to both sheep and birds, which can become entangled in them. I wonder how long I have before the gas company send an ultimatum!

Aside from the puyas I grow several other bromeliads, mostly in the cool, rubble-filled, brick piers of a low limestone wall. The first plants I tried were two forms of *Fascicularia bicolor*, whose spine-toothed, recurved leaves, dark above and silver beneath, form dense evergreen rosettes. From late July fist-sized heads of tiny tubular sky-blue flowers develop at the centre of the mature rosettes, accompanied by a startling change in the inner leaves which slowly turn from green to bright crimson. In the wild this plant grows epiphytically in trees and on rocks or cliffs. Once, when travelling in Valdivia, I saw a large tree in the distance full of what looked like birds' nests. On fixing them in my binoculars I realized that the nests were huge clumps of *Fascicularia bicolor*. Each clump occupied a crotch in the main branches and the larger ones must have been fifty years old, or more.

BOLD FOLIAGE PLANTS

Bold foliage is a feature of my garden, although with only a third of an acre or 0.1 hectare to play with, such plants must perform as individuals rather than in groups. *Schefflera impressa* is a shrubby member of the ivy family from the temperate rainforests of the eastern Himalaya. I first saw it forty years ago in a sheltered border at the Hillier Arboretum in Hampshire, and I have never forgotten the large, long-stalked, exquisitely divided leaves. Now I grow it here and although my three specimens are from different origins, not one has suffered in the past three winters. Being a forest subject, two of them are planted in sheltered, lightly shaded spots on a clay soil, where they grow vigorously on a single stem. The young leaves on two of my plants

◄ Puya alpestris, *a member of the pineapple family from the Chilean Andes, looks quite innocent in a pot display at Dixter, softened by companions such as feathery cosmos and hardy geraniums, but given space it will increase to 1.5 by 2m/5 by 6½ft.*

▶▲ *The hardy bromeliad* Fascicularia bicolor *is grown in the gutter on the north side of the house at Dixter. Christopher suggested planting a single, small rosette in a jiffy pot to get it established in a gutter or dry wall.*

have a bronze tint when they first emerge. Caught in the early morning or late afternoon sun, the effect is magical. Encouraged by their progress (the tallest is 2m/6½ft), I am experimenting with other, more recently, introduced species, just in case I get lucky.

On my first visit to China, in 1979, I was struck by the number and variety of palms I saw being cultivated in the parks and hotel gardens of Guangzhou in the southern province of Guangdong. I must have counted fifteen different species, large and small, and it had me fantasizing about how our own gardens and parks would change if we had a similar selection of hardy palms at our disposal. Since then a fair number of palm species have made their appearance, mostly in the warmer, coastal areas of Britain.

In my garden I have, for some years now, grown *Trachycarpus wagnerianus*, which is closely related to the more familiar Chusan or Chinese windmill palm, *T. fortunei*, differing in its smaller stature and much smaller leaves with stiffer segments that do not droop

at the tips. It is eminently suited to the smaller garden and, though it grows slowly, does not develop that ragged, hang-dog appearance so common in *T. fortunei*. The stem is equally wrapped in the dense fibrous remains of the old leaf bases, though this can be removed if desired and the fibre used to make a rough and virtually waterproof poncho, such as I have seen in China.

Despite having studied and admired numerous palms in the tropical areas of the world, including Malaysia and the Amazon, I have no illusions as to those which might succeed here. I have, nevertheless, planted three seedlings of the dwarf palmetto *Sabal minor*, which I recall seeing wild in Florida when visiting Disneyworld with my young family. There, it grows in swampy ground, which I cannot provide. But it is considered cold-hardy by some palm enthusiasts, so long as it is given a warm, sunny situation. For the adventurous plantsman this is evidence enough to give it a try.

Exotic PERENNIALS and SHRUBS

Clearly, a voluptuous exotic garden will need to embrace many plants that are not reliably hardy. Tender foliage and flowers help us create the illusion that, instead of being at latitude 51 degrees north, we are nearer the equator.

◀ *One of the great attractions in begonia leaves is that they are always eccentric, never regular, however varied their habit, colouring, shapes and textures. It is fascinating just to stare at and analyse a work of art like Begonia 'Little Brother Montgomery', especially when sunlight accentuates the leaf blades, which have about five deep marginal jags. Margins, centre and veins are dark, while the rest of the leaf is very pale and speckled. Given the right conditions (fertile, moist, well-drained soil and quite a bit of shade), this begonia may grow nearly 90cm/3ft tall and in October will surprise you with clusters of pale pink flowers.*

Immediate visual impact is what we want to create on entering the enclosed space of the Exotic Garden—once in, you're in the thick of it. As well as tender flowers, a wide variety of foliage plants, of many different shapes and textures, help us do this, and to maintain the effect through the garden's season.

Since Fergus Garrett came to me as head gardener, we have built three new greenhouses, all capable of keeping the frost out, one of them set to maintain a minimum temperature of 10°C/50°F. That is not high enough for some of the plants we would like to grow, but it gets a good many of them through.

The herbaceous American *Lobelia* are often lost during winter, so we lift stock at the end of the season and bed it in under glass, where little frost will enter. Then split and make more of the crowns of dormant shoots in spring. They like plenty of moisture. F_1 'Fan Scharlach' and 'Fan Tiefrot' are good seed strains, generally bright, pure red and the plants' habit is bushy, to 75cm/30in. One of the oldest is 'Queen Victoria', with long spikes of rich red flowers above reddish-purple foliage. Each crown throws up one stem to 90cm/3ft, so it needs support—one cane at the back and a single tie around each stem. It is most effective planted in front of a well-variegated strain of the grass, *Arundo donax* var. *versicolor*.

TENDER GRASSES AND GRASS-LIKE PLANTS

I wrote of the giant reed grass, *Arundo donax*, in my last chapter. The highly desirable *A. donax* var. *versicolor* needs to be treated with greatest respect, being, at its best, one of the most beautiful of all variegated plants, but there are snags in its respect. The white marginal leaf banding is its great attraction

▲ The tender broad-leaved grass, Setaria palmifolia, *makes surprisingly strong, wide-spreading clumps, becoming a fine specimen in a very short time. Drawn to fine points and with sharp margins, the surface of the leaves is handsomely ridged with parallel veins. However sick it looks after a winter under cool but frost-free glass, we allow for its spread when we plant it out. Once the weather warms up, there's no stopping it.*

▶ Arundo donax *var.* versicolor *in a well variegated strain where the banding of white is generously broad is the most luminous plant in the whole Exotic Garden. This grass will be 2m/6½ft tall well before the end of the season. Here it is echoing the arching shape of lower growing* Pennisetum setaceum *'Rubrum', whose coppery 'tails' droop from deep red stems and overhang the path throughout summer and autumn.*

but the width of this can vary greatly. When narrow, it looks quite undistinguished, but when broad, it will make this grass the most luminous plant in the whole Exotic Garden, or in any other area of summer bedding. One or two plants of it, widely separated by other plantings, will achieve the impression you are looking for.

However, the wider the banding, the less green remains in the rest of the leaf and this makes it far less robust or easy to propagate than a plant with plenty of green in it. Naturally, the nurseryman will incline to the course that makes life easy. The answer is that you must personally choose your own propagating material. If, in spring, you float an overwintered leafy stem on a water surface, it will soon root at every node, especially if the water is not too cold. These plantlets are then detached and treated individually, rejecting any that are less well variegated than you would wish. Even the weakest but most luminous plant that you may grow will be 2m/6½ft tall well before the end of the season.

Umbrella grass, an old windowsill plant, *Cyperus alternifolius*, is worth having in the garden during the summer and is usefully amenable to being grown in shallow water, say at a pond's margin. It lends an exotic touch.

We make important features of two tender grasses in our summer bedding. Fergus is particularly keen on *Pennisetum setaceum* 'Rubrum', both in pots for display and in the Exotic Garden overhanging the paving where it will create the greatest impression. He has learned how to manage it, lifting stock plants in their entirety, with as little root disturbance as possible, housing them in our warmest greenhouse, then splitting and treating individually when they start to grow, fairly late in spring. This way, the plants start to flower early and carry on with a succession of their long 'tails' — perhaps 50cm/20in long and drooping from 90cm/3ft stems — throughout summer and autumn. They are deep red and quite unlike anything else.

Setaria palmifolia has intense green, broad leaves with prominent parallel-ribbed veining. About 90cm/3ft high by the end of the growing season, it makes surprisingly strong, wide-spreading clumps and is always in striking contrast to whatever may be near it, but you must allow for its spread. That, again, we lift and house intact, in November. We are unable to prevent its looking sick unto death in the winter months but small signs of life remain at its base and in the centre of old clumps in the spring and these are treated individually. Once the weather warms up, there's no stopping them.

One of our favourite tender perennials is the Egyptian papyrus, *Cyperus papyrus*, with a mop of fresh green, thread-fine leaves crowning a tall (2.5m/ 8ft) naked stem. It looks particularly splendid beneath the banana leaves of *Musa basjoo*, being in striking contrast. To bring old plants through the winter is the devil, unless at a higher temperature than we can afford to provide. Luckily, seedlings are easily raised and when a year old, overwinter at a moderate temperature without difficulty. In the second year, they make fine garden plants, after which we start again.

▲ Furcraea longaeva *looks rather like a soft and flexible yucca, with an attractive blue bloom on the leaf that associates well with the metallic colouring of a* Eucalyptus gunnii *seedling, so long as that harmonious pairing is pepped up with some bright colour—here an apron fringe of single scarlet 'geraniums' planted in the gaps between its lowest leaves, and dahlias alongside. The furcraea's rosette of sword leaves grows larger each year, making overwintering an increasingly heavy task.*

◄ *The Egyptian papyrus,* Cyperus papyrus, *is easy enough to raise from seed but devilish to overwinter—a pretty high temperature is needed—and we always lose a proportion of our stock. In a season it will throw up numerous see-through stems crowned by a mop-like sphere of fresh green, thread-fine foliage that catches the light and makes a wonderful feathery foil to solid and sword leaves.*

SPIKES AND LANCES

Furcraea longaeva belongs to *Agavaceae* and looks rather like a soft-textured yucca, with an attractive blue bloom on the leaf. We turn it out of its pot for the summer, as it grows so much better in the open ground, but it has to be repotted for the winter and, as it grows larger, this becomes an increasingly heavy task. I told Fergus it would beat him, but of course it didn't. Our original plant came from West Hill Nurseries, near San Francisco. After six or seven years, it decided to flower. Great excitement! Its crown started to elongate as early as February. It rose to 2.5m/8ft or so, branched into a big panicle and was hung with small tubular flowers in green with hints of blue. Not showy but immensely exciting, after that long wait. Being monocarpic, it then died but it set some seed and, more to the point, it made hundreds of viviparous offspring. We potted a good many and gave away a lot more.

Beschorneria yuccoides is another member of this family and is hardy in really mild districts. Its leaves are similar to the last but it makes a number of crowns after flowering. Although the flowered one dies, there are others to take over. This flowers in May, which is really too early to be useful in the Exotic Garden, as it is nothing much to look at, at other seasons. We like to use it in our pot displays (see page 136), where it adds excitement for a few weeks. The inflorescence is thrilling, with large, bright pink bracts. The small tubular flowers are green and blue.

Yucca aloifolia has to be housed in winter but it is a most beautiful plant in 'Variegata' (correctly *Y. aloifolia* f. *marginata*), with a broad yellow central stripe and green margins. Some of the leaves curve inwards, some outwards. For such a sturdy plant, it has amazing grace.

Cordyline australis, the New Zealand cabbage palm, has narrow, spiky leaves radiating from a central woody stem like an exploding firework. In a cordyline trial at Wisley, they looked pretty dull en masse, in my opinion, but they are valuable solo incidents in mixed plantings. The striped cultivars, such as the pink, green and cream-variegated *C. australis* 'Torbay Dazzler', can be spectacular in the right place. Best, in my opinion, as solo incidents in mixed plantings.

A fascinating, but also beautiful, plant, *Thalia dealbata* associates well with cannas and dahlias. Growing to 1.8m/6ft or more in a season, its leaves are stylishly set at right angles to the stem. They are simple, 30cm/12in or so long and grey-green. The stem terminates in a raceme of quite tiny, inconspicuous flowers, interesting because they catch and ingest small insects. When the victim lands on a flower, which is attractively sticky, the stamens close over it and suck it dry, the skeleton then being discarded. This plant is water-loving. It will grow perfectly well in good moist soil but is also nice to see rising from shallow water at a pond margin. Rather surprisingly, *Thalia* self-sows and seedlings appear in the area where it was bedded out, in the following year. So there must be some degree of hardiness.

▲ Pseudopanax lessonii *'Gold Splash'* adds a touch of exotic pizzazz to a collection of pots at the bottom of the steps in the Blue Garden, alongside dahlias, begonias, rudbeckias and pelargoniums.

◀ *Low early morning sun shines on the small violet flowers of a stately* Thalia dealbata, *its wand-like stem rising high above leathery, heart-shaped leaves that are covered with a white waxy powder. This plant is water-loving, but grows perfectly well in good moist soil. Behind is lemon yellow Dahlia 'Glorie van Heemstede' in front of banana sails.*

FINGERED AND PALMATE FOLIAGE

With *Pseudopanax lessonii* we're back in the ivy family *Araliaceae*. The cultivar 'Gold Splash' is a handsome shrub to 3m/10ft or more (though easily kept lower), with large yellow splashes on its fingered leaves. Fergus, who lives within sight of the sea at Hastings, has kept a plant going for a number of years without special protection, but most of us either have to lift it in autumn or treat it as a pot plant. It will put up with quite a bit of shade and the gold splashing gives light to rather dark recesses.

At its best, *Trevesia palmata* (*Araliaceae*) is one of the most exciting foliage plants we can easily grow (though definitely tender). It is a solid shrub with deeply lobed palmate leaves, evergreen with a high gloss on them. Each leaf is up to 60cm/2ft across — not bad for an evergreen. Like others of its family, it doesn't want too hot a spot. When housed, it takes up quite a bit of space. To accommodate plants like this, we leave areas in the greenhouses where there is no benching. *Cussonia paniculata* (also *Araliaceae*) is another mouth-watering evergreen shrub with glaucous leaves and stems. Mine is looking unhappy. I think we closed it in too much. It is tempting, in an Exotic Garden, to jam-pack your plants. Bare earth at the height of its season is a disgrace. *Schefflera arboricola* (yet another *Araliaceae*) is generally seen as a house plant but is a tall, imposing shrub, excellent for bedding out. The leaves are palmate, not unduly large but well presented.

The leaves of Farfugium japonicum are quite thick, round, apart from a recess near the stalk, and shiny. F. j. 'Aureomaculatum' (in the foreground) has yellow spots of varying intensity, which it flaunts with panache. Behind is 'Argenteum', with leaves slashed with white across the green. Between these two bold foliage plants is the Japanese holly-leaved fern, Cyrtomium falcatum, and our great ally Begonia scharffii, with furry leaves and blush-white flowers.

ORBICULAR LEAVES

Euphorbia cotinifolia is a trap plant, so like a purple-leaved cotinus does it look, but it is far less bulky. The leaves are orbicular, not large, fleshy and beautifully veined. You can see it is a member of the spurge family, which makes us love it even more. Occasionally it produces some tiny cream flowers. Not at all vigorous, one is alarmed at the thought of losing it.

Farfugium japonicum is an evergreen perennial, which likes moist, rich soil and partial shade. I first saw it in Japan in October where it was revealing its membership of *Asteraceae* by flowering with rather common-looking yellow daisies. In Britain, our summers are not hot enough to bring it to this state before winter's arrival. In any case it's the orbicular leaves we want. Most beautiful for our purpose, in my opinion, is the 'unimproved' species, with plain, rich green foliage rising to no more than 30cm/1ft from the ground. Unfortunately, it is very slow to increase and is hard to get hold of. But most of its cultivars lend themselves to division.

My favourite of these is *Farfugium japonicum* 'Aureomaculatum'. In this the leaf develops large yellow spots. These are faint on first arriving (and their arrival is spread over a long period), but gradually intensify and brighten. It is a jolly plant. But often ridiculed for appearing to have been splashed with bleach. The more enlightened see its handsome qualities, as Fergus and I do.

The other variegated cultivar that we grow is *Farfugium japonicum*

◄ *Caribbean copper plant,* Euphorbia cotinifolia, *is a tricksy plant—irresistible and satisfying if you make a success of it. Like a* cotinus, *but without the wide elbows, its dark foliage is a perfect foil to variegated* Arundo donax *var.* versicolor *and silvery* Artemisia arborescens.

▼ *We grow tall* Eupatorium capillifolium *for its bright green feathery foliage, which is retained right into October, when such freshness is in short supply. It highlights almost anything you plant nearby and makes you pause for a while as you work out that it is forming a delicate screen between plantings.*

'Argenteum', whose leaves are boldly segmented with white. We leave a few plants to overwinter outside, placing a plastic-sheeted box over them in hard weather. Most of our stock is lifted in the autumn and overwintered under frost-free glass.

FEATHERS, NEEDLES AND ROSETTES

The purple-leaved euphorbia just cited comes from the Caribbean but contrasts splendidly with the pale grey, dissected foliage of *Artemisia arborescens* from the Mediterranean. I wouldn't call that hardy, though it not infrequently survives the winter with us, looking a wreck by the spring. Pruning should be circumspect. If you cut it back too early, you may lose the whole plant. Wait till you can see tiny shoot buds, low down on the old wood and cut back to them. Once it has got away it is very vigorous. Of course you can easily root cuttings in the autumn and overwinter them under frost-free glass, but a ready-established plant will be more imposing. This artemisia is also a great foil to purple-leaved cannas, notably the stylish 'General Eisenhower'. A. 'Powis Castle' is somewhat hardier and, being grey-leaved and fairly low, is a good foil to colourful begonias, for instance. It looks terrible by the spring but is restored, more often than not, after a good cut-back.

Eupatorium capillifolium is a tender perennial that occasionally scrapes through the winter but is best renewed from cuttings, annually, taken in late summer and overwintered frost-free. It is used purely as a foliage plant with

▲ *Perspiration on people is unattractive, but fresh and revitalizing on plants. When the Exotic Garden is steamy hot, Colocasia esculenta 'Black Magic', with its dark purple, soap-smooth and beautifully veined elephant's-ear leaves, starts to drip from its tips as early as 5 p.m. and continues well into the following morning.*

▲▶ *We use the bold, architectural Ensete ventricosum as punctuation marks in the Exotic Garden as well as in pot displays. This tender banana is better than Musa basjoo in a pot as it is bulkier and has a broader leaf with a bright red midrib that is worth studying close to. It has to be overwintered in a frost-free place.*

small, linear, bright green needle-leaves that retain their fresh colouring when most foliage has turned dull. The plant is narrow and shoots up to 2.2m/7ft quite quickly. If it flowers, you wish it hadn't, but really they're unobtrusive. It highlights almost anything you choose to plant nearby. It might be the castor bean, *Ricinus communis* 'Carmencita' (2.5m/8ft, if well fed and watered), which is the best seed strain I have found to date (see page 116).

The genus of bugloss is versatile. Just behind the tide line grows our native *Echium vulgare*, called viper's bugloss. It is biennial with 50cm/20in-tall spikes of funnel-shaped blue flowers including a hint of pink, as is the way of many members of the borage family (forget-me-nots, for instance). The main point of growing *E. pininana*, it seems to me, is for the bold rosette of foliage that it makes in the run-up to flowering. This Canary Islands species is monocarpic, flowering in its second or third year from seed. If allowed to flower, its spikes (a somewhat tarnished blue) rise to 4.5m/15ft and then seed prolifically. The flowering plant is certainly a talking point but it is grotesque, whereas seedlings transferred to the Exotic Garden will make a handsome feature in the year before they flower.

TENDER BANANAS

I have not had *Musa lasiocarpa* for very long, but it was a beautiful young plant on a salient corner where, when young, you could look down on it. Its characteristic banana leaves are neater than usual, stiff and upright. The Abyssinian banana, *Musa ensete*, is properly *Ensete ventricosum*, with paddle-shaped leaves up to 60cm/2ft wide and ten times as long. Ensetes make a single stem of indefinite growth and do not produce offsets. Each year that you house them, you are having to deal with a taller plant. However, it is easy to start again from seed, which germinates readily.

AROIDS

I terminate one end of a view through the centre of the Exotic Garden with a superb architectural plant, *Colocasia esculenta* (*Araceae*). It is called Taro in the markets, having edible and succulent tuberous roots. But it is a most ornamental herbaceous plant. You can store the tubers in winter as you would tuberous-rooted begonias. This, on a plant 90cm/3ft or so tall, has large, perfectly smooth Ace-of-Spades-shaped leaves. Far from looking coarse, they are exquisitely poised on long, soft stems and they swing in the wind. The smooth surface readily accumulates dewdrops at night, which drip off the sharply pointed leaf tip. I once, in the early morning, saw a toad sitting under one of these and evidently enjoying its shower bath. The leaves are delicately and intricately veined. There are several cultivars, of which 'Black Magic', with dark purple leaves, is one of the most striking. But we find it none too easy to grow well.

HOUSE PLANTS AND OTHER SHADE LOVERS

I got the idea of running the Cape primrose, *Streptocarpus*, through other shade lovers, ferns and low begonias, from seeing them treated as bedding in Australia. I planted out the blue 'Constant Nymph' (30cm/1ft), one of the smaller-flowered varieties, in partial shade when the nights had warmed up. It took quite a while to settle down, but was glorious in September.

At a low level, begonias are the principals but I will first draw attention to a little *Impatiens* (yet another member of this versatile genus), *I. pseudoviola*. As its name suggests, its growth and flowers suggest a little white violet. It was given me by a friend in Cheshire, who bedded it out, but as she well understood it is totally tender. Easy from summer cuttings.

A PASSION FOR BEGONIAS

Begonias, which have a world-wide distribution in warm temperate and tropical areas, are a huge subject. I remember that Maurice Mason, with acres of garden near Kings Lynn in Norfolk, devoted an entire greenhouse to them, most of the contents collected by himself, he and his wife Margaret being great travellers and used to hard conditions, when need be. He was as generous a gardener as you will find and always sharing his plants.

▶▶ *High summer means high drama. The great shovel-shaped leaves of colo-casias have grown like the clappers in the three months since they were planted out in June. Their stalks arise from ground level and, when the wind blows, the leaf blade swings from side to side. It is smooth and with a swirling, feathery venation, drawn to a fine point at the tip, which points downwards. The feather palm,* Butia capitata, *with long, arching, blue-green fronds, stayed out all winter in Bed 7, unprotected—a risk worth taking since we got away with it.* Ricinus communis *'New Zealand Purple' with dark red, palmate leaves was sown at the end of April and is now 2.5m/8ft tall, while dahlias, begonias and cannas provide bright colour.*

65

▶ Begonia boliviensis *has a profusion of bright orange-red flowers on succulent red stems.*

▼ *The palm leaf begonia, B. luxurians, has leaves divided into long fingers, presented in more or less of a circle except, when you look closely, for the give-away begonia lopsidedness. New growth emerges from the centre of the next oldest leaf.*

▼▼ Begonia scharffii (B. haageana), *with dark, furry leaves, reddish on the undersides, surpasses itself as a flowering plant, with large, loose panicles of shell pink blossom.*

)

Fergus and I have a passion for begonias. If we were reduced to growing only one genus, that would be it. They have so much to offer — from small and compact to tall and scandent; flowers and, above all, fantastic foliage with incredible variation in the colour and markings. Most are happiest with quite a bit of shade. All have a give-away lop-sided (asymmetric) leaf shape that you'll find in no other genus that I know of.

Some have normal fibrous roots; others have tubers. Tuberous bedding begonias, which are especially popular for bedding out in the north of England and southern Scotland, dry off entirely in the winter and are easily stored in a cool, dark place. You can bring them out in early spring and start them again into growth in damp peat — not wringing wet, just damp — and they'll want little or no watering for a while, until they have put out new roots. Then they can be transferred to a potting compost and, as their growth becomes stronger, given more water. Eventually they are hardened off for whatever purpose they are needed.

This type of begonia has been much developed for showing purposes, most prized being those with huge double blooms of silken texture and incredibly easily damaged. For years, Blackmore & Langdon have brought them to Chelsea together with their famous delphiniums. Very expensive for them but it would be a shame if this kind of exhibition art were lost.

We have nothing to do with any of this at Dixter and the heat and space we can supply or spare is modest. One of the few tuberous kinds we grow is an old cultivar, 'Flamboyant', with small single red flowers on a compact plant. That goes into a pot display outside our entrance porch. 'Panorama Orange' and 'Panorama Scarlet' are both truly small-flowered, weeping hanging basket types, but they are perfectly suited to bedding out, as many weepers are. 'Illumination Orange' is another such.

In a trial of bedding out, Semperflorens-type begonias on the RHS trial ground at Wisley, most had been bred for dwarf compactness, which I think removes all individuality, but then if you want a carpet of bedding plants, individuality is not what the breeder is after. However, in this trial was one called 'Stara White', with a little height and personality, and it is the one we went for.

I should hazard (Fergus isn't here to ask) that *Begonia luxurians* (1.2m/4ft) is the one we most admire. We like to get it on the shaded side of a yet taller dahlia, on its south side, this being the pastel mauve Waterlily dahlia 'Porcelain'. *B. luxurians*, exceptionally, has leaves that are divided into long fingers, presented in more or less of a circle except, when you look closely, for the give-away begonia lopsidedness. However could that have happened? you can't help wondering.

B. scharffii (syn. *B. haageana*) is a splendid all-purpose species. It has furry leaves, green on top, reddish underneath. Its blush-white flowers contribute pleasantly, too. The plant is rangy in habit. Given a stake, it will rise to 60cm/ 2ft or more. Of an obliging disposition, we find it a great ally and an excellent

▲ *Given a juicy, organic-rich soil and, in many cases, a spot of shade against the hottest July sunshine, begonias will reward you for months. We tuck some in when putting the beds together but then, as the season progresses and the canopy lifts, shady spaces open up and we add another layer. The large-leaved 'Marmaduke' (left) has a mosaic pattern in copper and lime green. Puckered 'Burle Marx' has recessed veins (centre). Deeply jagged 'Little Brother Montgomery', again (right). After being turned out of the greenhouse and of their pots, it may take the foliage types a few weeks to settle down.*

filler in many situations. I like to have a potted plant of it on my dining room windowsill in winter, where it performs non-stop. Sometimes it gets embarrassingly tall. In many cases it is difficult to give heights for begonias as so many of them are ready, literally, to rise to a challenge.

'Marmaduke' was for years a favourite in his house of a friend living in the heart of London. But it is excellent for our purpose. A fairly broad leaf of pale green background colouring but heavily splashed and speckled reddish brown. It shows up well.

'Burle Marx' makes a lowish bushy plant of quite solid appearance. Its broad leaves are of a uniform, dark green but with a heavily, uniformly puckered surface. Symmetrical, as begonias go. The recessed veins of the upper surface are prominent on the underside, which is reddish, but not normally visible.

MORE FAVOURITE BEGONIAS

Of every begonia we look at, we're apt to say that's my favourite. Certainly of 'Little Brother Montgomery'. The leaf is deeply jagged with long points, dark green at the centre and on the margins but with a pale pattern, this paleness being interrupted by dark veins which create a rather mottled effect. In the course of a summer outside, it may grow nearly 90cm/3ft tall and is notably arresting. Right at the end of the season (October), it will surprise you with clusters of pale pink flowers.

B. metallica is capable of growing quite tall. The light-reflecting leaf surfaces further draw attention to themselves through the deeply recessed veins, which break up the shiny surface. The pale pink flowers are of secondary importance. *B. maculata*, whose clone 'Wightii' is the more widely offered, has a slim, olive green leaf, handsomely interrupted by gleaming white spots, randomly scattered, up to a 6mm/¼in across or slightly more.

Any selection of begonias one may make must be both random and inexhaustibly selective. We first knew *B. masoniana* as 'Iron Cross', which is a bit deceptive, as the cross has five, bifurcating limbs, but the name gives the right impression, as the leaf shows a strong contrast between its green background and the strongly patterned dark design that overlays it. Maurice Mason, a great plant hunter in the tropics, brought it back from Singapore, its homeland being Vietnam and adjacent parts of China (Guangxi). The plant is bushy, not climbing.

We have only lately acquired 'Escargot' from Dibley's and look forward to trying that in the garden. A large leaf with a dark-light-dark green design. Tapering to a point, the leaf broadens at its base and its lobes, near to where it joins the petiole, project and curl, in a manner reminiscent of a snail.

The bushy 'Hot Tamale', bred by Tovah Martin (a great begonia specialist) in the USA, has lance leaves with well displayed, rich red undersides. It has a long and telling flowering season, the flowers being pinky-red. 'Ebony' is classified as having cane-like growth, growing 60cm/2ft high in the garden (depending on the height at which it started). Lance-leaved, the upper surface is uniformly dark green but the well displayed underside is rich red and glossy. Pink flowers.

Of the many begonias grown for their flowers, one that we find most satisfactory in quite deep shade is Dragon Wing Red ('Bepared'), of which we buy in tiny plantlets in the spring. They soon grow and give us, at 50cm/20in or so, a very long display.

What I have written about this genus can only be sketchy at best and it should be subject to violent fluctuations of content. I hope I have made clear, through its many facets, why this is so. Also what a joy all the experimenting is.

▼ *No apologies for yet more begonias, a group of plants that has everything the heart could desire.* Begonia metallica (left) *is an old favourite with dark green-veined leaves overlaid with a metallic gloss.* B. maculata (centre) *has slim, olive green, bat-wing leaves, handsomely interrupted by gleaming white spots, randomly scattered.* B. *Dragon Wing Red* ('Bepared'), *with scarlet flowers and glossy green foliage* (right) *is wonderful for lighting up quite deep shade.*

Dan Hinkley

BIG COOL LEAVES

Plants exotic, by definition, are not of the place we garden. They have the capacity to transport us to somewhere unfamiliar and flamboyant.

BEING, like Christopher, a gardener of the temperate northlands, where our endemic foliage shrinks predictably as we head towards the pole, there is nothing like large leaves to take me on a visual adventure. To some people exotic may mean steamy combinations of colours, overpowering fragrance or jagged, intricate texture. At Dixter exoticism is multi-layered. To me it simply means big.

MOISTURE LOVERS

An extremely hardy plant that gets relatively little attention is a Manchurian candidate, *Astilboides tabularis*, which was once amalgamated with the genus *Rodgersia*. It needs a moist, partially shaded position in the garden. In generous soils, the matt green rounds of foliage (superficially, to my eye, replicating those of the lotus) can extend to 60cm/2ft across. They are attached centrally to their leaf stalks which rise to 90cm/3ft in height. Its growth habit is politely spreading, if not somewhat down tempo, a trait that, in the end, always makes for a happier, lasting relationship. There are clusters of white flowers on stems rising above the foliage which make a predictable and, fortunately, brief appearance in early summer. Should they not appear for some reason I would lose little sleep. I have seen this plant growing in exposed sites in Anchorage, Alaska, so its hardiness and adaptability are unquestionable, though I find it more appropriate, visually, in a glade.

With more sheen and less substance than *Astilboides* is *Darmera peltata*. As the epithet implies,

it too has leaf stems which meet its blade in the centre lifting them to 1.2m/4ft throughout summer. The thick, knobbly rhizomes creep above ground and it is directly from these that very pretty pink flowers on tall stems appear in spring, long before the foliage buds have considered unfurling. In time the flowers are usurped by quickly expanding, fluted leaves which, after several seasons of patience, will fill a respectable quantity of airspace during the summer. I first admired this species in the Sunken Garden at Sissinghurst in Kent and later found it growing in its native soil, in and along the shaded streams of northern California. My admiration of this plant comes by way of its depth of talent: in shade or sun; perpetually moist or moderately dry, its performance is consistently good.

COOL CUSTOMERS FOR SHADE

Collectively known as the May apples, podophyllums, in particular the species introduced from China, are splendid herbaceous perennials possessing the most arresting foliage of all plants, hardy and otherwise. *Podophyllum pleianthum* carries a pair of rubber-textured, glistening green leaves with an overall shape reminiscent of a starfish. The leaves, up to 38cm/15in across, do not give the impression of being deciduous, until late autumn when the plant finally collapses into dormancy. *P. veitchii* is very similar in appearance. *P. delavayi*, on the other hand, emerges in tones of mottled purple on a green satin background, distinguishing itself as one of the most beautiful plant introductions in modern horticulture. In a cooler climate it retains these seductive qualities throughout the growing season.

The drawback of the Asian species of May apple, despite its ephemeral nature, is the disagreeable odour of the blood-red flowers, produced from the leaf stem below the leaf blade. As with most plants that produce aromas we associate with a beef roast gone over, the chief pollinators are flies. Though they do not spread as vigorously as the American May apple, *P. peltatum*, the Asian species will form colonies of stems over time.

Sharing a fleetingly similar appearance, and a

close cousin, is *Diphylleia*. The name means two leaves, and a triad of species exists, one each from China, Japan and eastern North America. Of these, and with no bias, the American wins the beauty contest hands down. From shady, moist ravines in the south Appalachians, *D. cymosa* produces stems to 90cm/3ft, each carrying very large, jagged-edged leaves to 45cm/18in across. Unlike podophyllums, the clusters of white flowers are produced on stems above the foliage, resulting, in late summer, in arresting crops of colourful fruit, ripening to an opulent white-washed sapphire blue just as the flowering stem matures to coral red. Though not particularly dependent on moisture, it desires a shaded position.

The woody aralias of North America and Asia are well known and admired, particularly in their variegated forms which, though still pricey, have become increasingly available. The herbaceous members of this species, of which there are many, are the poor

cousins, but worth every bit as much for ornamental effect. *Aralia cordata*, from eastern Asia, is remarkable in the sheer amount of growth it produces, with mounds of long, pinnate foliage rising to 3m/10ft or more in a single season before retreating to ground level upon the first frost. There are elegant sprays of white umbels, swarmed by bees and wasps in late summer, resulting in pendulous swathes of purple fruit. A flamboyant golden-foliaged variant of this species has been recently introduced from Japan and should be sought out.

ENTICING PRICKLES AND FRONDS

There are few hardy plants that offer such absurdly large leaves as *Gunnera*, the prickly rhubarb. *G. manicata*, from Brazil, which is the species growing by the horse pond at Dixter, and *G. tinctoria*, from southern Chile, have been shown off in cultivation for well over a century. Though requiring moist feet to propel it to full potential, *Gunnera* is not a servant to boggy soils. Indeed, the most abundant and luxurious stands of *G. tinctoria* are found growing in beach sand along the coasts of Chiloé Island. The fanciful cone-shaped flowering stems, up to 90cm/3ft, only add a few exclamation points to an already implausible appearance. The natural distribution of *Gunnera* hops across the islands and continents of the southern hemisphere. It is *G. perpensa*, from moist mountain valleys and meadows throughout the Western and Eastern Cape in South Africa, that I find particularly appealing. The annular foliage, atop stems up to 90cm/3ft tall, is very finely toothed along the margins, curling in on itself like a wickedly wavy green sea. It too is tolerant of sun and moderately moist soils.

Equally enticing are the hardy tree ferns, in particular *Dicksonia antarctica*. With fronds unfurling in spring in a controlled explosion of finely fretted green, atop trunks that ultimately reach 2.5m/8ft or more, the effects conjured are a cross between tropical beaches and the landscape of Brontosaurus. It is

◀ *A finely fretted green frond of* Dicksonia antarctica, *the soft tree fern from the forests of eastern Australia, Tasmania, and some sub-Antarctic islands. In winter Fergus covers the crowns with bracken to protect the uncurling croziers and stipes, which are covered with soft, reddish-brown hairs.*

◀ Blechnum gibbum,
a miniature tree fern from Fiji
with light green, palm-like fronds,
is nurtured in a pot at Dixter.

▲ Gunnera manicata *develops*
vast leaves that engulf the flower
head, which is conspicuous
in May, and remain bold and
beautiful until the first frost.

probably hardier than most people realize. The fibrous trunks of *Dicksonia* are the means by which water is absorbed by the plant and must be regularly watered in the summer and the winter alike. As an extra precaution in winter the trunks may be wrapped with insulated plastic foam, though the top must allow water to penetrate. One can nestle dried bracken over the crown to provide insulation to the terminal bud, while still allowing the percolation of rain water.

Much hardier than *Dicksonia*, the evergreen *Blechnum chilense* (from Chile) provides luscious, leathery, deep green fronds up to 90cm/3ft long,

emerging in spring in tones of ruby red. This plant appreciates a rich soil where it can spread by stolons creating, over time, considerable colonies.

With a more finely crafted frond, but equally hardy and ground-covering (perhaps with a bit more grace) is the genus *Woodwardia*. The Asian species, *W. unigemmata*, is widespread from Taiwan, across China and into the Himalaya. It makes a plumed fountain of leathery-textured fronds of up to 2m/6½ft long. Small plantlets are produced at the end of each leaf, which can root and carry on the colony. Somewhere in the reaches of my memory are scenes of this species cascading down moist, shaded, vertical cliffs in northern Sikkim. It would be a sensational way to employ it in the garden, especially if one's moist, shaded, vertical cliffs have yet to be planted.

CANNAS
and DAHLIAS

The canna's simple, paddle-shaped leaves contribute firmness to our plantings, the dahlia's foliage is generally mundane (pinnate, like a potato's) but their flowers epitomize summer's full glory. They are perfect team players.

Canna and *Dahlia* are the principal genera providing the Exotic Garden with brilliant — though not necessarily brilliant — colour from June to October. They are among my favourite tender perennials, not only going well together but also combining well with other plants, and both have a range of impressive forms.

Cannas hail from tropical and warm temperate Central and South America. Their first wave in popularity coincided, in the mid-19th century, with the installation of heated glass in private and public gardens. When heating became too expensive, they went into eclipse, though were never entirely abandoned in the public sector. I believe I may have been partly instrumental in reviving interest in cannas during the post Second World War years, but most have been propagated and distributed in and from the Netherlands.

This is the reason for the rapid spread of a new and disastrous virus disease during recent years. Dormant tubers distributed to our nurseries from the Netherlands were infected and it was everywhere. This was just at the time when a canna trial — the first ever — was being conducted at Wisley. The virus rapidly spread not only through European stock but into clean American stock, notably from Longwood, that had been sent over for the trial. Each of us needs to be vigilant for tell-tale signs of the disease, in leaves, stems and flowers, destroying infected plants the moment trouble is spotted.

Cannas, if disease does not rear its head, are easily managed in much the same way as dahlias. After the top growth has been frosted, we cut the plants down. The dormant rhizomes can be stored in darkness during the winter in old potting compost, kept just damp enough to prevent shrivelling. We visit them fortnightly and give them a thorough watering if the soil has nearly

◀ *The stripy-leaved cannas are quite something, especially with sunlight behind them. Most self-proclaiming is 'Phasion', also going around by other names including 'Durban' and Tropicanna. The leaves are purplish but striped bright pink. Get plenty of lush foliage around these cannas and they will blend in perfectly well, but they are best sited at a border's margin, where their entire height can be savoured.*

77

▲ Canna 'Striata' holds its leaves, boldly striped green and yellow, more or less upright and makes a contrasting backdrop for Lobelia cardinalis 'Queen Victoria' with reddish-purple stems and leaves and long spikes of pure, volcanic red flowers.

◀ Best of the tall, purple-leaved cannas in the Exotic Garden is 'Wyoming', which has large, brilliant orange flowers (see page 23). We get our cannas into mixed plantings of a similar mood and roughly similar stature, and make bold groups of several plants of the same variety together.

▼ Canna 'Louis Cayeux' is a deep pink, green-leaved canna that gives excellent value. Here it looks good near Phormium 'Sundowner', which has pink stripes in its sword leaves.

dried out. In spring, we bring them out, at our leisure, when there is space available in our deep cold frames and we use no artificial heat at all. When sprouting strongly, we pot them individually, breaking up the rhizomes if we wish to increase stock.

TRANSLUCENT LEAVES AND SHOWY FLOWERS

Canna indica is the species from which most cultivars have been developed. In its own right, it is popular in its purple-leaved variant 'Purpurea'. It grows 2.5m/8ft tall and has obliquely upright foliage that allows translucence, most effective when the sun is low, early and late in the day. We plant a large patch of it each summer on the margin of our mud-bottomed Horse Pond, where it makes a striking feature. It won't stand having its crowns actually submerged. Two lower-growing (1.8m/6ft) cannas share the asset of translucence even more effectively. Both have striped variegation, 'Striata' in green and yellow, 'Phasion' (Tropicanna), like 'Durban', in a subtle range of pink and purple colours, but with orange, not red, flowers.

While some cannas are grown entirely for foliage effect, in others the flowers provide the main display. These, especially in our capricious climate, are at the mercy of the weather and collapse into a mush under adverse conditions. But they can provide a grand display. One of the showiest, in my experience, is 'Louis Cayeux', with salmon-pink flowers in abundance. 'General Eisenhower' would be my choice for all-round excellence. Purple-leaved, it has a proud and stylish habit before ever a flower appears. It looks great, for instance in front of a planting of the grey, filigree-leaved *Artemisia arborescens*. The flowers are strong red.

A rather differently styled canna not to be missed is the hybrid *C. × ehemanii*, sometimes incorrectly known as *C. iridiflora*. It has large, lush green leaves with a thin purple margin but the flowers are the thing. Instead of the usual upright raceme, the inflorescence bends over gracefully and is a delightful shade of cherry red.

Ever intent on dwarfening tall plants, the Dutch aim in their breeding work to produce showy-flowering, low-growing cannas fit for the patio. They cannot have the presence of the tall kinds, one of the tallest seen around being *C.* 'Musifolia' — well named banana-leaved, perhaps 3.6m/12ft high. It seldom flowers in our climate and the flowers are insignificant anyway.

There is an interesting group of water-loving cannas, which will also thrive in any damp soil, but it is a special joy to see them rising from shallow water in or at the margin of a pond. They derive from the pale yellow *C. glauca* — my stock came from Argentina. This has given rise to a whole group of similar water lovers in different colours and developed at Longwood Gardens in Pennsylvania. The salmony 'Erebus' is a prolific flowerer.

'Mystique' is grown for its purple with green, translucent leaves, held rather upright. Quiet but satisfying. So the canna offers us a surprisingly wide range of beauty and interest.

The cannas you can grow in shallow water do equally well on terra firma. Canna 'Erebus' derives from the prototype, C. glauca, *but has an even bluer leaf and salmon pink flowers. Here, at the end of September, it is making a good show in Bed 8 with* Dahlia 'Porcelain', D. 'Admiral Rawlings' *and the metallic foliage of* Eucalyptus gunnii. *It also does well in a pot in my Sunk Garden pool. Remember that cannas are exceedingly greedy and need a really nourishing compost. Their thirst is well-nigh unquenchable, once they are growing strongly, but go easy on the water when they are coming out of dormancy and before they have a strong new root system.*

▲ *This beautifully shaped Waterlily dahlia, 'Pearl of Heemstede', is a clear, unadulterated pink. It has an elegantly informal look and is good with* Verbena bonariensis *and purple* Solanum rantonnetii.

DAHLIAS FOR ALL TASTES

While I fell in love with the sheer flamboyance of cannas in a public park in Nairobi, in 1945, I think I became smitten by dahlias through Harry Stredwick, who bred them in Hastings, not far from my home. Although he superficially seemed crusty, he hit it off with my mother and me, and his much younger wife was a dear. He called one of his Giant Decoratives 'Daisy Lloyd', after my mother, and she was proud to be photographed standing next to it on a Wisley trial.

Till recently, now that it is appreciated what good garden plants they are, I suppose all dahlia aficionados were chiefly interested in them on the show bench, which meant the largest possible Giant Decorative blooms, each individually nurtured and heavily disbudded so as to attain just a few enormous blooms. Fergus joined the Dahlia Society and was given a range of these Giant Decs by a member of the old school. For lack of space in his own tiny garden, he grew them at Dixter. He did a little disbudding—not very much— and the results I have to admit were very beautiful, especially as cut flowers.

We revel in dahlias at Dixter. For a time I gave them up in my mixed border plantings, more from anxiety over wind damage than anything, for we are exposed on our southwest-facing slope. Plus a bit of laziness, I do admit: there's the 'trouble' of overwintering the tubers and starting the plants in spring, whether you replant the same tubers or rejuvenate them from cuttings; then there's staking and tying; and also capsids and earwigs need controlling. Since Fergus came to Dixter in 1993, however, we've been into dahlias in a big

There is no season when cuttings may not be made but in the warm half of the year plants are active and in a cooperative mood. Late-struck dahlia cuttings have fresh leaves and fresh flowers right through to the end of the season.

- *Take cuttings from a vigorous stem, avoid flowering shoots if you can.*
- *Trim off the tip.*
- *Trim the stem below a node (joint).*

- *Remove the flower bud, if necessary.*
- *Trim to leave just two pairs of leaves; dip the stem in hormone rooting powder.*
- *Use a dibber to insert cuttings around the edge of a pot filled with 50:50 damp cutting compost and grit. Be sure to label them.*

way, and they are ideal in the sheltered Exotic Garden, providing a succession of brilliant colour. We wait to get overwintered tubers out of storage in April so they'll be just the right size for planting out in the second week of June. By then they will have started to sprout so it is quite a hairy business. Overwintered tubers start to flower in early July and start to slow down come September. All it takes is bad weather (a wet September), and a bit of botrytis to set in, and the whole plant can lose its vigour. So we also take late-struck cuttings (early May with us) that will peak in September and remain fresh right into October (frosts permitting). As regards varieties to grow, there are dahlias for all tastes. You should visit the trials at Wisley to appreciate the range. Some of the mini-types are quite revolting, in my opinion. The one variety that even the snobbiest of gardeners will allow some credit is the

‘Moonfire’ (in the foreground) is a single-flowered, two-tone dahlia which has a vibrant effect, here with Canna ‘Wyoming’, Dahlia ‘David Howard’, Kniphofia linearifolia, Arundo donax var. versicolor and Eupatorium capillifolium—all leavened with white Cosmos bipinnatus ‘Purity’.

Single-flowered Dahlia coccinea (a form that Mary Keen gave us) with Canna ‘Musifolia’, which we grow purely for foliage effect—immense green banana-like leaves (though not as large as a banana's) with a purple margin and veins.

red-flowered, dark purple and quite dissect-leaved ‘Bishop of Llandaff’. And it is nice, though I've grown a bit bored with it. One of the dahlia’s endemic problems is its foliage, which is generally rather plebeian and uninspiring. So if it can be dissected or interestingly coloured, it gets marks for trying.

POPULAR DAHLIA TRENDS

The public’s tastes are forever shifting and the current trend is towards informality. Single-flowered dahlias are definitely chic. Back in the 1940s I regularly bedded out with single-flowered Coltness hybrids (60cm/2ft) in mixed colours. I notice in the trials that singles are being bred to have blooms tilted upwards so that on plants 90cm/3ft or so tall, they seem to be giving you a welcoming smile. However, the strain of D. coccinea that I am growing, with single red flowers, is 1.8m/6ft or more tall and the blooms are tilted downwards, just as needed. ‘Moonfire’ (90cm/3ft) is popular and in that the petals shade from pale apricot at the perimeter to bronze at the centre. All open-centred dahlias set masses of seed and need dead-heading every three days or so, both for appearances’ sake and to encourage the production of

more flower buds. Dead-heading is itself an art, the cut needing to be made right back to where the stem branches and the next flower bud is located. If done sloppily, so that snags are left behind, it sets your teeth on edge — or should do.

Collerette dahlias are currently a popular class. Inside the main outer ring of petals (I should write rays) is a ring of shorter rays, often of a different colour or of two colours partly including that of the main frame. 'Chimborazo' (1.8m/6ft, named after a volcano in Ecuador) is one such, in red and yellow. 'Clair de Lune' (1.8m/6ft), by contrast, is a Collerette of the same soft yellow right through the bloom. One year we had this with *Verbena bonariensis* and the effect was electrifying, each helping the other, colour-wise (see page 89).

If we are bored with 'Bishop of Llandaff', which red dahlias are we to grow? I think highly of 'Grenadier' (1.5m/5ft), myself. A small, prolific, almost globular dahlia that normally gets going in late June. But it will peter out before late autumn. You can sidestep this by propagating it from cuttings rather late in spring, say in early May, but its total length of flowering season will remain the same.

▲ 'Grenadier' is a thoroughly reliable and early starting, pure red Small Waterlily dahlia, which glows in morning sun, here in September with Canna 'Wyoming' beyond.

▼ Dahlia 'Wittemans Superba' (1.5m/5ft) has substantial, deepish red blooms borne on strong stems and presenting themselves proudly.

One of our favourite reds is the Small Semi-cactus 'Wittemans Superba', because there is interesting shading in its colouring, the backs of the rays being purplish red. As these are most visible in the centre of this fully double flower, the whole bloom presents a gradually merging two-toned effect.

The ideal two-toned dahlia, especially effective with back-lighting, is the Medium Cactus 'Hillcrest Royal' (1.8m/6ft). It is magenta, but two-toned with more of purple in the centre. Any photographic reproduction of this cuts out the blue element entirely, so that it looks uniformly red all through.

Perhaps the most popular of all dahlias, and deservedly so, is 'David Howard' (1.8m/6ft). (I keep meeting people called David Howard and always ask if they are any relation, but they look blank.) Classified as Miniature Decorative, it is not that small. It has an incredibly long flowering season. As it increases in height, producing more of its apricot-orange blooms all the time, it conceals those that have faded, which anyway shed their petals, so that it is almost unnecessary to dead-head it—more than I could say of any other dahlia.

One of our (Fergus and my) favourite dahlia classes is the Waterlily type. These are fully double but with fewer rays, giving the bloom a relaxed appearance. There is a good range of them in the trials. 'Porcelain' (2.2m/7ft) is especially beautiful, with a pearly mauve flush to a bloom that refuses to be white. It is disinclined to make good tubers, for winter storage purposes, but Fergus says he has the measure of its foot. Pot tubers are the usual solution to

▶ Dahlia *'David Howard'*, with dusky orange flowers and purplish leaves, has a tremendous capacity for keeping up its abundance of bloom for month after month.

▼ *Medium Cactus* Dahlia *'Hillcrest Royal'* is vibrant magenta but photographs cut out the blue element entirely, so that it looks red all through.

▲ *One of the oldest favourites is the pale yellow dahlia, 'Glorie van Heemstede', which makes splendid contrast to mauve* Verbena bonariensis *and lights up recesses formed by* Cyperus papyrus. *Behind is* Acacia pravissima, *with a branch succumbing to a soil-borne fungus, which we had to remove.*

this problem. You grow rooted cuttings in quite small pots, don't allow flowering and the root restriction encourages the production of tubers which overwinter easily and provide material for cuttings in the following spring. Quite a palaver, you may say. *Il faut souffrir pour être belle.*

'White Ballet' (2.5m/8ft) is a pure white Waterlily that we use in the Exotic Garden as well as against the dark yew hedge at the back of our Long Border where it brings light to a rather shady place. On the whole I'm not enthusiastic about pink dahlias but 'Pearl of Heemstede', clear, kind pink with no mauve in it, must be an exception.

Dahlia 'Glorie van Heemstede' is the most popular of all Waterlily types — a bright yet kindly yellow. The bedding dahlia 'Fascination' (60–90cm/2–3ft) is described not very appropriately as a Waterlily; it makes a quite startling impression with bold, pinky-mauve flowers set off by bronze foliage. Another good bedder is 'Ellen Huston' (60–90cm/2–3ft), again with dark foliage setting off orange, semi-double flowers. It has the merit (unless you live in a frost pocket) of getting into its stride late, looking fresh when much else is jaded.

D. imperialis is a one-off species for foliage effect, a real jungle plant that deserves plenty of feeding. It grows to 2.5–3.6m/8–12ft in one season and is often hardy enough to be left *in situ* through the winter. Where you need a big foliage feature, this is the one for you. Flowers come just before the first frost but are of no account anyway.

I have written nothing about dahlias left *in situ* from one winter to another, though this is a practice popular with many gardeners. It quite often works well enough though it indicates a kind of sloppiness that does not appeal to me. Apart from severe frost, the danger, especially on heavy soils, is from slugs. Also, the Exotic Garden changes from year to year and we like to create our jungle every June from a clean slate. Still, if you have no storage facilities...

▶ *A good companion for* Verbena bonariensis *is the pale yellow Collerette dahlia, 'Clair de Lune', a single which has a pale yellow collar of smaller rays.*

▶ ▼ *The tree dahlia,* D. imperialis, *has rich foliage and long, hollow stems which, apparently, were used by the Aztecs to pipe water from mountain springs and streams. This exotic-looking freak of nature makes rapid growth if given plenty of organic matter and water.*

A MAGICAL COLOUR EXPERIENCE

Andrew Lawson

With colour, as with so many other things, Christo wore his heart on his sleeve. To get an idea of his preferences you need look no further than his choice of casual shirts. Decked out in canary yellow, turquoise, or pillarbox red, Christo was an ornament in his own garden.

ON ONE OCCASION at Dixter I was taking photographs in the Exotic Garden when I saw Christo approaching, deep in conversation with Fergus. They took ages to work their way through the garden, discussing each plant grouping in turn. This gave me plenty of time to get myself into position to take a portrait. I knew that Christo didn't much like having his picture taken (who does?). I wanted to get set up and ready before asking him. To compose the picture I took my cue from the colour of his shirt. That day it was a brilliant lilac one. So I lined up with a clump of *Verbena bonariensis* to make a foreground. The flower colour was an almost perfect match for the shirt. When he and Fergus reached my position, it was a matter of seconds to frame the portrait and take the picture.

I was quite pleased with the result (it appeared as the cover of the American edition of the revised *The Well-Tempered Garden*). But I knew that matching Christo's colour scheme with an adjacent plant was contrary to his approach to colour. He rather despised the whole idea of colour theming to create harmonious effects. He never really saw the point of matching plants by colour to make single colour groupings. He called such schemes 'polite' and 'appallingly good

taste'. Such ideas were far too safe for him. He wanted colours to be provocative and stimulating. For him, colour presented endless opportunities for excitement. You can see his passion for contrasting colours everywhere in the garden at Dixter. And it is in the Exotic Garden that his contrasts are most daring and appropriate.

The orange and cream flowers of *Ipomoea lobata* (syn. *Mina lobata*) wrap around the lilac bobbles of *Verbena bonariensis*. The near-turquoise leaves of *Eucalyptus gunnii* are a foil for the deep carmine *Dahlia* 'Hillcrest Royal'. The flowers of the different cannas are like droopy silk pocket handkerchiefs of scarlet, orange, primrose and pink. These colours, suspended high above the ground, stand out like traffic lights against the muted terracotta tiles of the hovel. This old farm building, with its walls of sun-baked wooden slats, makes a frame on the north side of the Exotic Garden. The house itself is set further back on the eastern side, but it acts visually as another side of the frame, its silvery timbers and mellow brickwork contrasting with the bright colours of the garden and rendering them all the more fresh and intense.

Whenever I discussed colour with Christo we would have a friendly disagreement about one colour contrast that he rather liked and which I find troublesome. He often put together yellows and pinks, both in the Long Border and in the Exotic Garden. For me the combination is uncomfortable, because of the 'coolness' of most pinks (apricots are a bit different) in contrast with the 'hotness' of yellows as well as of reds and oranges. The effect also has to do with the dilution of colour in pale pinks as compared with the fully saturated hues of yellows and oranges. There are mid-pink dahlias in the Exotic Garden, and also a rather pasty pink rose, *Rosa* 'Chanelle', which I suspect he kept as a memento of the rose garden that was here originally. I never summoned up the courage to tell him that, in my opinion, the colours of the Exotic Garden would be all the more intense without these pale pink flowers. Christo did concede in writing that 'I don't grow many pink dahlias — it is a difficult colour to get right'. But of course it wasn't in his nature to banish any plants that he was fond of.

Especially if somebody had criticised them.

In the British Isles our native flora tends to be restrained in colour and modest in display. What's more, we commonly see our landscapes under the dim light of overcast skies and through an atmosphere diffused by humidity. As a true Englishman, Christo appreciated the subtle effects of English nature, as the meadow at Dixter demonstrates. But he realised that the most effective way to create an exotic effect in the garden is to put together plants with properties that are at opposite extremes from our own. So he mainly used plants with flowers that are large and bright. The same goes for foliage. Our climate favours a haze of narrow-leaved grasses and trees and shrubs with small or divided leaves. So Christo went for plants with enormous leaves, such as the paddle-shaped ones of *Musa* (banana) and *Canna* or spear-shaped like *Arundo donax* and *Yucca*. As for their colour, the huge variety of greens and purples in the foliage makes

a big contribution to the exotic atmosphere of the garden. Add the saturated reds, oranges, yellows, lilacs of the flowers and the overall colour effect of this small enclosure is like a fireworks display. Every time you go from the adjacent meadow through the narrow yew entrance into the Exotic Garden, you realize what a magical colour experience Christo has created.

▼ *A fireworks display in early October 2003. To either side of relatively sober grass-like plants, orange-and-cream flowered* Ipomoea lobata *wraps around lilac* Verbena bonariensis *on the left and* Dahlia 'Wittemans Superba' *on the right. Behind are banana paddles and D. 'Bishop of Llandaff', with dark-leaved* Ricinus communis *and* Eupatorium capillifolium *rising high to form a screen in front of the hovel's tiled roof.*

SUCCULENTS
and a few cacti

Succulents play an important part in the Exotic Garden, having a bold style of their own. 'We are very important plants', they tell us and they are right. Their fleshiness gives them a settled, no-nonsense look.

Clearly succulents are designed for a special habitat. It is generally exposed to all the sunshine going, hot, possibly windy, generally dry. Not too frosty, although if the freest drainage is there, they will often put up with far more cold than you would expect. My garden's dour clay is anathema to them, so we have to lighten the soil as best we may and choose the most arid and sunny sites we can. There they can form a community, contributing a flavour poles apart from begonias and ferns and yet, surprisingly, not geographically distant at all. Like most of the Exotic Garden, the succulents spend two thirds of their year in the greenhouses and do not venture forth into the open air until early summer, where they will remain till October.

Our concentration of succulents, with a few cacti among them, is in the hottest and sunniest bed (Bed 5 in the plan on pages 18 to 19) and in the two, rather sober, grass panels on the Lutyens steps that lead from the lower terrace down to the Orchard and the Exotic Garden. We wanted somewhere to plant out more cacti and succulents so for the last couple of years we have been lifting the turf here and replacing it with these ultra-exotics. They enjoy the open, south-facing aspect and the gritty soil (made gritty by Fergus for their benefit). He plants them out (wearing stout gloves) after the last frost, with plenty of grit around their skirts to help drainage and stop their bases rotting. Their delight is indicated by the fact that many of them double their size in a matter of months. When we have built up enough stock, we shall experiment more freely with hardiness, especially of the opuntias.

◀ Prickly pear-type cacti in the hot, well-drained beds on the Lutyens steps, with sun highlighting the barbed bristles. Fergus once carried one of these opuntias home clasped to his chest. He was extracting prickles for the next week.

PRICKLY PEARS

The succulents in the dry, baking area of our Exotic Garden largely comprise opuntias, fast-growing cacti of widely varying shapes and sizes, popularly

▶ The steps leading from the lower terrace down to the Orchard and the rose garden, seen here in 1955. They were designed by Lutyens in 1912 and, while aubrieta was encouraged on the walls, the circular grass panels retained their sobriety until 2004, when they were replaced with cacti and succulents, bedded out for summer, as a prelude to the exuberance of the Exotic Garden.

▼ After the last frost, Fergus plants the cacti and succulents in the beds on the steps. 'You can't go wrong,' he says, 'if you consider their contrasting shapes and textures as you place them. They've all got different characters which speak for themselves.'

▶▶ Many succulents never see the light of day except through glass, but given a summer airing, such plants create an open-air oasis of colour, texture and luxuriance. We are delighted with the way their muscularity has transformed the steps.

▲ Opuntia robusta *flowering outside in August.*

▶ Opuntia falcata (*syn.* Consolea falcata) *from Haiti has flattish dark green stems and segmented branches spotted with small beige tubercles. This one, recently acquired, has yet to enjoy a summer outside.*

known as prickly pears. All cacti are American (though many have become naturalized in other parts of the world). The distribution of *Opuntia* is from Utah in the north, where they are subjected to winter frost, to Patagonia in the south of South America. Many come from Mexico and Arizona.

Those that tolerate frost are able to do so on account of extremely dry conditions in winter. Suitably sited, with full exposure and drought at the root, a surprisingly large number of species are hardy in Britain. There are half a dozen of opuntia perfectly happy in an exposed position in the London zoo. They often thrive along our coasts. There are upwards of 300 species (many of them disputed). You shouldn't imagine that they require no attention. They need renewing from time to time, planting up with small pieces. Some can be grown from seed.

Opuntias create an atmosphere. Often it is one of depth. Their pads face in different directions, catching the light in varied ways, sometimes flat and straight on, at others slanting, so that there is a great play on light and shade. Stood in containers on a windowsill (this should only be temporary) they are beautiful in silhouette. They have a big range of shapes. The one we call Wide Boy, spreads outwards leaning on its elbows and rooting wherever a branch touches the ground. It looks relaxed and pleased with itself, in contrast to a species of upright habit and long spines. Always beware touching any of these as extracting the prickles is not easy and takes a long time.

Opuntias are varied in structure and size, not infrequently making trees. The few I have, are not all named. You tend to pick them up from private sources. One pair was bought by Fergus at our village flower show. Their previous owner had clearly found them too vigorous. One of these turned out to be *O. subulata*, with cylindrical stems. Some have flat pads and an upright habit. Such is *O. robusta* (Mexican), with big pads. Its flowers are yellow, though not large or numerous. However, some opuntias draw attention to themselves with vivid red and magenta flowers.

When I came upon a flowering opuntia in the wild, it was near Denver, in Colorado. It was low-growing and had flowers wide open to the sun. Intensely exciting, I have to say. This was in an area of winter frosts whose damaging effects were nullified by the low humidity at that season.

The surface of the pads is peppered over with little protuberances, called glochids, which are barbed bristles that replace the original tiny, short-lived leaf. This is notable on a dwarf species, *O. microdasys*, whose popularity largely derives from its diminutive size being in such contrast to many others and enabling the owner to study it at close quarters. Its pads are thick with glochids and are most attractive.

When we plant our succulents and other exotics for the summer we turn them out of their containers so that they have a free root run and they go mad with joy (to be anthropomorphic). The opuntias are no exception. The difference between their appearance in June and the growth they have put on by October is amazing.

▶ We bring Agave americana 'Marginata' out of the cold frame as early as we dare, and have been experimenting with leaving one outside in a sheltered spot by the teahouse, which so far has survived. It gives solidity to whatever scene—borders, pot displays (here with the small, brown-centred yellow daisy, Rudbeckia hirta 'Toto') and the cacti and succulent beds. Where safety dictates, we remove the sharp points from the agave's leaves—although they look so handsome, they are a bit of a hazard to the unwary.

▼ Agave parryi is a succulent that builds a rosette of fleshy leaves for years (this one is fairly young); when it decides it is time to flower, it throws up a huge phallic spike that grows with almost visible speed.

FLESHY AGAVES

Agaves can make very large, impressive plants, as anyone who has seen them on the Mediterranean seaboard (to go no further) will testify. Projecting from the cracks in rock faces suits them admirably. Even in England's seaboard resorts, they can make themselves look remarkably at home. There are generally a few large crowns and a great many pups of differing sizes. Many leaf colours and patternings are available.

One of the most important-looking is fittingly named *Agave victoriae-reginae*. It has dark, fleshy leaves of great substance. Each leaf is tipped with a long, black spine but leaf margins are narrowly rimmed in white and there is a very thin white design on the broadest areas. Strength with delicacy.

Where agaves can grow big, they are impressive, eventually flowering, that crown subsequently dying. *A. attenuata* is called the Swan's neck agave, the yellow-green flowers twisting like a swan's neck. They make big rosettes that look impressive poking out of cracks in walls. Like many succulents, they are subject to overwatering. In the garden where Fergus was employed in the Côte d'Azur, the owners insisted on a green, English-style lawn. This went against the climate but they had to have it. But the dry-loving plants around, which caught the spray, couldn't stand it and died.

The Ruth Bancroft Garden at Walnut Creek, in the Bay Area near San Francisco, has an amazing succulent garden, the core of which consists of gun-metal-grey *Agave franzosinii*, better, I was told than the commoner *A. americana*. It had a spacious area to itself, surrounded by dirt (their word) and they make an impressive colony that extends by rooting into the bare ground. A village of agaves, their shadows giving that familiar feeling of depth. What seemed particularly extraordinary about that garden to me was that it also included conifers and deciduous trees and many plants that were not succulent, although there were communities of opuntias.

AEONIUMS

Among the succulents, other than cacti, that we plant out for the summer are *Aeonium*, a sub-shrubby genus largely native of the Canary Islands, where they grow on cliff faces. Some of them make very large, fleshy rosettes of foliage, for which I consider them more valuable than their flowers. These come in panicles and mine are all yellow.

Most impressive of mine, as I write, is *A. tabuliforme*, which is stemless with flat rosettes of overlapping, pale green leaves margined with tiny white hairs. The rosettes are perfectly circular and impressively large. This is a meal in itself and the tall, branching inflorescence seems, visually, superfluous, though the effort of making it will kill the plant off. Unlike other aeoniums it is not easily propagated from cuttings, so you must either work from seed or acquire the cristate form, which throws off rosettes both straight and crested.

For some years we have used *A. undulatum*, a statuesque shrub of great green heads on stout stems, the eponymous undulation being on the leaf

▲ *A hot, sunny bed that we keep on the dry side is just what a planting of cacti and succulents enjoys. This is Bed 5 on the plan (pages 18–19), which is where we had a concentration of these exciting plants before making a place for them on the Lutyens steps. Here, in 2000, is the opuntia we call 'Wide Boy', and other prickly pears with neat pads which contrast so strikingly with the fleshy rosettes of* Aeonium arboreum *and purple-leaved 'Zwartkop'. Towards the front there are crassulas,* C. perfoliata *var.* falcata *and* C. ovata. *Glaucous* Cotyledon orbiculata *makes a solid feature and, spreading across the path, is a blue-fingered* Senecio mandraliscae.

◄ *Almost black* Aeonium 'Zwartkop' *in a pot display with silvery white* Centaurea cineraria.

margins. Of equal, if not greater, vintage to us is *A. arboreum* 'Atropurpureum', which can be of similar stature, with smaller rosettes of luminous near-black. We now grow *A.* 'Zwartkop' instead, which is darker still, and the line is blurred where one faded out and the other took over. 'Zwartkop' is more brittle and more difficult to grow into a large plant. Recently a friend introduced us to *A.* 'Cyclops', a hybrid of *A. undulatum* and *A.* 'Zwartkop', with the size of the former and much of the blackness of the latter.

'Zwartkop' has also been crossed with the demure *A. simsii* (so demure it was once thought to be a *Sempervivum*) to produce a nice branching shrub with numerous rosettes, flushed dark purple. It is one of those aeoniums that likes to get about on its elbows, hirsute with optimistic roots. It seems to go, unimaginatively, by the name *A. simsii* × 'Zwartkop'.

In *A. canariense* the rosettes are loose, soft and deep. They can be enormous. Mine are not. It is a branching shrub of some size and great character, with glaucous heads facing this way and that. The leaves are spoiled by the slightest frost. That exception aside, aeoniums in general are tough and easygoing

plants. Breakages become instant cuttings, with no need to callous the wound as with other succulents. Neither do they like to be kept completely dry in the dormant season, although they will tolerate it. The dark kinds darken with sunlight and, come the autumn, are a good indicator of what kind of summer we've had.

ALOES AND OTHERS

There is an elegance about many of the aloes that belies their substance. The leaves are often arched and pointed, the flowers lofty candelabrum. Some are obligingly and surprisingly hardy, most notably *Aloe striatula* which, in time, makes a large mound of toothy pennants. Extreme cold and wet will make a black and foul-smelling mess of it, but clear that away and new shoots should appear from underground not long after you've given up hope.

A. breviflolia survived several winters in Fergus' garden in Hastings. It also has a certain, congested, charm to recommend it. Forms seem to vary inexplicably. That may be a matter of cultivation. The suckering form of *A. saponaria* seems to multiply like aphids, making ever-thickening mounds of dark green stars flecked with white. It too can shrug a dry winter off, without much bother. Perhaps the most beautiful aloe of all, *A. polyphylla,* is said to tolerate a blanket of snow in its Drakensberg homeland, but who would be foolish enough to test it, out of curiosity? It is a translucent spiral of asymmetrical, overlapping pyramids, if you can find one.

A tree aloe, such as *A. barberae* or *A. plicatilis,* would be the ultimate, if you could think of a way to overwinter it at maturity. Meanwhile, as juvenile plants and for as long as they can be managed and man-handled, they are worth their weight in trouble. Shrubbier *A. arborescens* or *A. ferox* might prove more manageable in the long run, though the latter can live up to its name and put up a good fight at lifting time. It is always astonishing, when taking aloes out of the ground, how much root growth they will have made in a season. Long monocotyledonous whips of deepest yellow thrash out of the soil in all directions, tensing and snapping as you wrestle the beast.

Succulents that are glaucous or bluish make an important contribution to a scheme which will not rely on flowers for colour variation. The great broad pads of *Cotyledon orbiculata* are almost silver and have the sweetly dolorous quality you would expect from a pachyderm. South African *Senecio mandraliscae* (syns *Kleinia mandraliscae, Senecio tabinoides* subsp. *mandraliscae*) is more upbeat. Thick copses of blue fingers spread into the light, throwing themselves carelessly across the path. Echeverias come in greys and blues also, but perhaps most interestingly in pink, in the lush *Echeveria* 'Perle von Nürnberg', which is suffused with an inner glow. A strong red can be had by planting *Crassula capitella* 'Campfire' in starved soil, as we did one year on an awkward corner on top of the wall above the upper moat.

◀◀ *In a terracotta pot made locally to us at Gopsall Pottery in Winchelsea Beach, Echeveria 'Elegans' steals the show among fuchsias and agaves.*

▲▲ Cotyledon orbiculata (*given to us by Beth Chatto*) *has large, rounded pads that are almost silver. These comprise an admirable group, once settled in.*

▲ Aloe mitriformis *makes rosettes of toothed, lance-shaped leaves.*

▶ *This tall and bristly, columnar cactus has been identified as* Echinopsis pachanoi *by Greg Redwood of the Royal Botanical Gardens, Kew.*

Stephen Anderton

RUBBING SHOULDERS WITH PLANTS

Christopher Lloyd's Exotic Garden, so trend-setting since it was created in 1993, is fresh and delightful but at the same time essentially traditional. How dare I speak such heresy? Let me explain.

WHEN THE KINDS of plants Christo used were being introduced in the late 19th century, they were loud, shocking novelties compared to our accustomed European flora. Think parrots when you have always lived with blackbirds and you get the picture. Like exotic birds and animals in aviaries and zoos, the Victorians caged them in. Some they paraded in bedding schemes, but the most alien and dangerous plants were segregated in island beds where gardeners stood bananas next to palms next to cannas, chaining them at the ankles with lines of spider plants and celosias and securing them safely behind little wire fences. (Go to Waddesdon Manor in Buckinghamshire and see the recreated Exotic Mound: the craftsmanship is superb.) This was plants as spectacle, to be stared *at*.

What Christo did so remarkably at Dixter was to liberate those plants. Yes, they are still hemmed inside the hedges of the old rose garden, but once you enter the jungle you can walk *amongst* the plants, *under* the plants, rub shoulders with them as you never could when you were staring at a fenced island bed. That is the point of the Exotic Garden and it is an entirely different relationship.

Christo made no bones about mixing exotics from wet and very dry climates and somehow, practically, it worked. What mattered to him was the look of the thing, and that persuaded him to include any plant which was extravagant in its architecture and colour, whether from wet or dry habitats; it was (to change the metaphor) a kind of asylum for all plants so flamboyant that they might have caused a disturbance in the rest of the garden. And so dasylirions stood facing *Musa basjoo* across the path, and a hop and a spit from opuntias were black, tip-dripping colocasias. Call it mad but it worked.

Keeping those two palettes of plants happy together for half the year is a huge but invisible compromise and difficult to manage. The solution is to provide a rich moist soil, heat, and shelter which, given super-sized helpings of muck and lashings of water, the old hedged rose garden was able to provide. To the hot-and-dry lovers it felt like a holiday at the Ritz. To the hot-and-wet lovers it felt like a pleasantly comfortable Three Star hotel.

But it is precisely because the hot-and-wet lovers were out of their preferred conditions that they could be used in a controlled and sophisticated English garden. At home in their accustomed tropical heat and high rainfall, they grow at a furious pace. Bananas make new leaves faster than Californian women exfoliate and the old ones hang there, raddled and shabby (the leaves, that is); palms drop dangerously large chunks of bristly debris as the leaves and flowers expand; evergreens drop leathery leaves all summer. When these fast-living plants are grown in England they still need to be kept tidy but the turnover of foliage happens at a slower pace; there is opulence without shabbiness.

HARDY GROWERS

It is that same pace of growth which makes temperate-climate plants such as *Paulownia* and *Acer negundo* 'Flamingo' look right in the Exotic Garden: when they are pruned hard and richly fed they grow like the clappers. There is similarly conspicuous pace in the great grey reed, *Arundo donax*; you can almost feel it growing, leaves thrown back in the slipstream.

Acer 'Flamingo' tells a useful tale. It was exoticness of colour combined with bold, well-fed foliage that made Christo put a plant into his Exotic Garden, even if it came from a cold native climate. 'Flamingo' has outrageous (some would say frivolous) variegation and was allowed in. *Phormium cookianum* subsp. *hookeri* 'Tricolor' is included for its long striped leaves even though it loves cool wet conditions, especially if it is to remain pest-free; I have seen it thriving off the Irish coast on a rock a few metres across. Drought-tolerant *Verbena bonariensis* is there, but so are moisture-loving dahlias and thirsty cannas, even

varieties derived from *Canna glauca* which naturally grows in shallow water and was used that way in Christo's Sunk Garden.

Christo wanted his Exotic Garden to be fresh and fun, 'a little piece of make-believe,' as he put it, as if 'a magic carpet had transported us somewhere like Wagner's magic garden in *Parsifal*'. And so now, as you push through the extravagant foliage and flowers, you are engulfed in a delightful, giddy atmosphere that occurs nowhere else in contemporary English gardening. Some people of course might have done things differently; there are no rules, as Christo would have admitted.

▲ *A view from the hovel, inviting you to step from shadow into bright light, to leave thoughts of the elegant topiary garden behind and enter the jungle, to push through extravagant foliage and flowers and rub shoulders with flamboyant plants, both hardy and tender, moisture-loving and drought-tolerant alike.*

ANNUALS
and infillers

The joy of annuals and bedding plants is that you can change your mind with impunity. 'Look at us while we're around,' they seem to say in a gather-ye-rosebuds sort of way. 'We'll be gone soon.'

We use annuals and other short-lived plants in several ways in the Exotic Garden: showy flowers and foliage plants to stop gaps in the under storey, annual climbers to thread through shrubs and perennials in need of pepping up and the corn marigold to make us smile. Pouring over the new season's seed lists, it's safe to indulge in thoughts of experimenting, but for the Exotic Garden we must avoid plants that set seed by July and be sure to choose subjects that have a long flowering season.

SELF-SOWERS AND OTHER LINKING PLANTS

The short-lived perennial *Verbena bonariensis* is a great favourite with us and makes a linking thread through the Exotic Garden for nearly four months. It self sows with abandon and we have to edit its myriad seedlings to keep it from dominating the scene—indeed, in warmer countries it can be a nuisance. We love the clusters of mauve flowers atop tall (2m/6½ft), wiry stems that form see-through screens for more sophisticated flowers and foliage. They also act as supports for annual climbers (see below). The plants last no longer than two or three years, but they generally survive the winter with some old growth intact, which hastens the onset of flowering.

The verbena contrasts with another favourite self-sower, the corn marigold, *Chrysanthemum segetum* (60cm/2ft), which we now have to call *Xanthophthalmum segetum*. The leaves are grey-green and the daisy flowers a bright, clean yellow. We delight in leaving some of the seedlings to create a haze of fresh colour around cannas and dahlias and beneath the skirts of foliage plants. They are past their prime by the middle of August, so we pull them out as the season progresses. The marigold is often the only yellow around in the Exotic Garden.

◄ *Annual climbers make wonderful fillers to clamber over other plants and you can find room for them without having to think of special siting. Ipomoea lobata (syn. Mina lobata) is a favourite with us. It can do virtually what it likes, investigating neighbouring plants but without harming them, and its short chains of tubular flowers, which change colour as they age, from white, through yellow to orange, enhance whatever host it may choose.*

▲ We can't resist trickling some Ageratum houstonianum 'Blue Horizon' through the Exotic Garden to form an understorey with begonias beneath Rosa 'Chanelle'.

▶ *Favourite self-sowers.* Verbena bonariensis *makes a pierced wall of green stems and heads of soft purple flowers from July to October. It is a see-through plant, not seriously blocking the view beyond. Still, we have to be strict with it, weeding out 99 per cent of its seedlings (see page 149) and often cutting plants halfway back in mid-season. It goes on flowering till the end of October. Or seems to. Sometimes it's a case of the old plant gradually giving up, in September, but being superseded by young stock, which does the carrying on. With us there is always an army of young Turks jostling to take over. The verbena contrasts with our other favourite self-sower, the bright yellow corn marigold,* Xanthophthalmum segetum (syn. Chrysanthemum segetum)*. This germinates easily and we thin the seedlings in May, leaving some along the edges and underneath shrubs. We pull out any that turn out to be in the way as we plant cannas and dahlias. If you allow too many corn marigolds to stay, they crowd each other out and, when they are finished (mid August onwards) and you have to pull them out, they leave too much of a gap.*

White-flowered *Nicandra physaloides* (2.5m/8ft) is a hardy self-sower and looks strange but not beautiful. It may just turn up but is not worth bothering about except as a curiosity.

Common or garden nasturtiums are a great asset, though their behaviour certainly wants watching. The endearing thing about them is that they have ideas of their own and wander off to investigate other plants in other parts of our borders. I write about the unimproved *Tropaeolum majus* with its familiar nasturtium red colouring. It has tenacious longevity and will self-sow with abandon, once introduced. Seedlings need constant thinning. It has a climbing habit and can be especially useful against a north-facing wall, which suits it as well as any other aspect. Many colour strains have been developed, most of them bent on softening the uncompromising scarlet that comes naturally to it. In the exotic garden it needs strictly controlling, else it will take over completely.

Persicaria orientalis (syn. *Polygonum orientale*) (2.5m/8ft) has the strange habit of needing cold to break its dormancy but then of needing warmth to get it going. Its seeds are hardy and self-sowing. If you try to start them with heat, they just won't have it and you will wait in vain. So we let seed from previous years germinate in the borders; then pot some of them up and bring them on in warmth. The pink flowers, quite late in the season, come in drooping racemes but you need to rub them between your hands in order to make them release their shiny black seeds. Where summers are warmer, it can be quite a weed. We don't have that trouble and rather enjoy it but it does need staking.

Certain long-flowering annuals are particularly good for creating links that connect different parts of a planting. They can be threaded through perennials to create their own themes. *Ageratum houstonianum* 'Blue Horizon' is one such — showy and very long flowering. Ageratums have been messed around by the breeders with the idea of making them as dwarf and compact as possible, but they lose all individuality in this way. 'Blue Horizon' at 60–90cm/ 2–3ft retains this. It has quite a spraying habit but you may have to scratch around a bit to find it. Sometimes you may have to resort to a wholesaler, which makes it expensive, because you'll be buying far more seed than you actually need. We sow masses of 'Blue Horizon' from mid April to the beginning of May for planting out in June.

COSMOS AND CO

Most of us like to include *Cosmos bipinnatus* in our borders but they are awkward in several ways. They are naturally short-day plants, flowering when the days are twelve hours long and tending to make a lot of unproductive greenery during the long days of our north latitude summers. Their seed for our markets is largely grown and harvested in short-day countries like Kenya, so there is no way of knowing how they will behave when they find themselves in long summers day countries like ours (it is actually the length of night that

▲ Cosmos bipinnatus *'Sonata White'* has a leavening effect in the Long Border, its feathery stems contrasting with the dwarf golden bamboo, Pleioblastus viridistriatus, *the huge elephant ears of* Colocasia esculenta, *and purple-leaved* Dahlia *'David Howard'*.

really counts). A few years ago there was a *Cosmos bipinnatus* trial at Wisley which was a fiasco. The plants grew so enormous that you couldn't move among them but they had scarcely any blossom at all.

However, there are strains of cosmos that can be relied upon, especially the Sonata Series. *Cosmos* 'Sonata Pink' is good with *Ageratum houstonianum* 'Blue Horizon' in the Long Border but needs a weightier companion in the Exotic Garden, such as *Canna* 'Erebus' (1.2m/4ft), which is among the most versatile of its kind, with grey-green foliage that is slim and upright and flowers of a pleasing shade of salmon. That's saying a lot, because salmon is not one of the easiest colours to be fond of, in my estimation.

'Sonata Pink' also goes with *Salvia involucrata* 'Bethellii' (2m/6½ft), which is fairly late flowering and quite a loud — you might, unkindly, call it vicious — shade of pink with a dash of mauve. Other possible partners include the delectable *Arundo donax* var. *versicolor* and *Dahlia* 'Hillcrest Royal', which subtly combines red and purple in a combination that is never reproduced in colour printing, as the blue element is invariably lost.

Cosmos 'Sonata White' needs a dark companion, as it might be *Canna* 'Mystique', whose slim, upright purple leaves are its main point, the tiny red flowers amounting to nothing. Popped in alongside the tender grass, *Pennisetum setaceum* 'Rubrum', with long, purple spikes that arch under their own weight, 'Sonata White' has a leavening effect. Try it, too, with the taller lobelias, as it might be 'Queen Victoria', with purple leaves and red flowers, or 'Fan Scharlach', with green leaves and brilliant scarlet flowers.

▼ *The velvet purple-red plumes of* Amaranthus hypochondriacus *have great presence, reaching 2m/6½ft in a good season.*

▼ ▶ *Amaranthus cruentus 'Foxtail' has upright flowerhead 'tails', but the main point of the plant is that it is suffused throughout with crimson, which shows up well in front of the metallic blue juvenile leaves of* Eucalyptus gunnii. *We sow some amaranth under glass in April but we wait until the beginning of May to sow the plants we intend to use in the Exotic Garden.*

ANNUAL FOLIAGE

The main point of the annual *Amaranthus* is to have a variety in which the whole plant is suffused with colour, although the tassels are fun, too. *A. hypochondriacus* and the similar 'Foxtail' (1.2m/4ft) have a tall, spraying habit and go well with *Canna* 'Erebus' (1.2m/4ft) — slim, glaucous leaves, salmon flowers — *Dahlia* 'Fascination' (1.2m/4ft), which is a fairly recent favourite, with bright pink flowers set off by purple foliage, and the rather yucca-like *Furcraea longaeva*, whose glaucous leaves are flexible. The tall (2.5m/8ft) but airy Egyptian *Cyperus papyrus* would also blend well. *Arundo donax* var. *versicolor*, in a well variegated strain, would be irresistible. Able to set any of these off is *Eucalyptus gunnii*, with leaden foliage. You need juvenile plants, whose leaves are completely different and a lot more interesting than the mature, as I described in the chapter on hardy and structural ingredients.

Kochia, the so-called burning bush, is now *Bassia scoparia* (80cm/32in). It is cone-shaped and a very bright green which, even in the seed strain called 'Evergreen', turns magenta right at the end of its season. It is good with dark canna foliage. We saw it at Merriments with not only dark cannas but also the green-and-yellow-striped *Canna* 'Striata' and a young palm — a surprisingly effective team. It is easy to find partners for fresh green foliage, as it might be *Dahlia* 'Bishop of Llandaff' or 'Grenadier'.

Helichrysum petiolare has felted, heart-shaped leaves on an obliging plant of rambling habit, much used for hanging baskets but an excellent weaver at or around ground level. It could be in striking contrast investigating the red-flowered, purple-leaved *Canna* 'General Eisenhower', but it also tumbles out of ornamental pots and conceals hard lines. The lime green version, *H. petiolare* 'Limelight', is apt to scorch in strong sunlight, and should be sited accordingly. Begonias enjoy the same conditions. A classic combination used at Sissinghurst Castle in Kent is with the prolific apricot *Begonia sutherlandii*. We should hear a public outcry were it not to be used there. The public is very bossy and stick-in-the-mud about changes in the gardens with which they are familiar. Change for the sake of change is a bit childish but should certainly not be resisted if you want to try out something new. Retaining the status quo because that's the way it's always been done, is just an excuse for not thinking afresh. Annuals and bedding plants are the best material for experiment, because alterations are so easily made and mistakes corrected.

The ornamentally crimped parsley called 'Bravour' makes a beautiful undulating three-dimensional plant in brightest green and there is no question of its running to flower in its first year, so it looks as fresh in autumn (often in contrast to surrounding plants) as it did in summer. Fine for garnishing, no doubt, but I shouldn't dream of actually eating it. That's not the point, anyway. Bright green right through to autumn is to be treasured and it contrasts strikingly with a single-flowered dwarf orange French marigold, 'Disco Orange'. The parsley also combines well with the red lobelia 'Queen Victoria' and with the purple arum leaves of *Colocasia esculenta* 'Black Magic'.

You seldom, these days, see *Coleus* bedded out. *Coleus blumei* we used to call it, correctly *Solenostemon*. Some strains have curiously crimped leaves. I prefer those whose leaves are plain in outline, but the design is on the leaf itself. What we do with these at Dixter is to sow a batch of mixed seed in small pots, in early spring. When the seedlings are large enough to see what's what, we select the ones we think promising, throwing out the obvious duds. Coleus make good pot plants and we keep some for that purpose. They will come in for pot arrangements, which Fergus is good with, either side of the entrance to our porch and in other key positions that seem to need pepping up.

In other years we bed them out on the northwest side of an old shed which is known as the hovel. Fergus brings me a large batch of seedlings and, after discarding the boring ones, I arrange them in groups that I think will associate well with one another and we thereafter bed them out. They hate the cold, so

◀ As you leave the topiary lawn and are about to duck beneath low beams to enter the hovel, the planting in this northwest-facing bed gives an inkling of the magical jungle you will enter on the other side. Being cool, it is the ideal spot for Solenostemon, *better known as coleus hybrids, which enjoy the afternoon sun. We sort them by colour and leaf patterns before planting out in July.* Eupatorium capillifolium *forms a light curtain of bright green between the coleus and the permanent backdrop of* Hedera helix *'Buttercup'.*

we don't do this till quite late—end of June, perhaps, and they make a good follow-on to some biennial whose season was May–June. Once established, they grow enthusiastically and will still be at their best when an October frost puts paid to them. They may go on even later than that, but by then we shall want to bed out with something for the spring.

We use *Verbascum bombyciferum* not as a flowering plant but for its rosette of grey foliage at a border's margin. Similarly, *Echium pininana* and its close relations have a role solely for their glamorous rosettes of silver-grey foliage in their first year from a March sowing. They become rather grotesque when flowering in their second, but there is no need to wait for that. They look good when combined with succulent foliage plants, as it might be opuntias, but also with bigger plants like *Tetrapanax papyrifer*, which looks tender but is surprisingly hardy, or with *Colocasia esculenta* (called taro in the Chinese markets) or its dark-leaved cultivar, 'Black Magic'. It could even vie with bananas, like *Musa basjoo*, caught in the year before they want to run up to flower (which ruins them as foliage plants).

Ricinus communis is the castor oil plant and I should hardly need to say that it is poisonous, though we are unlikely to want to eat it. 'Carmencita' grows to 2.5m/8ft in the right conditions; its palmate leaves are dark red, while its stems and seed heads are a brighter shade of red. You can sometimes save your own seed but be ruthless when sorting out the seedlings in the following spring, choosing only those with the darkest leaves. As we have little heat on offer, we don't sow till the end of April, when there is plenty of sun heat in a close, cold frame. Preserve the heat by spreading a mat or suchlike, over the glass at night.

The strain called *Ricinus* 'Bright Red' is one of the most ornamental, with red stems and bright red burrs, which are the young seed capsules. That looks good with the tall (2.5m/8ft), purple-leaved *Canna indica* 'Purpurea'. Its colouring is on the same wavelength, which makes the contrast in leaf shape (elliptical in the canna) the more striking. To pep the scene up, you might use a dahlia, like the apricot-orange 'David Howard', or the reddish-purple 'Hillcrest Royal'.

The ricinus also looks good with the stately *Canna* 'Musifolia' (3m/10ft). Also, a little surprisingly, with the blush pink Decorative dahlia, 'Pearl of Heemstede', with 'David Howard' and 'Wittemans Superba', red with a purple flush near the flower's centre. It also goes with the Egyptian papyrus, *Cyperus papyrus* (up to 3m/10ft), with *Musa basjoo* and the juvenile foliage, leaden in colour, of *Eucalyptus gunnii*.

▶ Castor oil, Ricinus communis, *in dark red and green-leaved forms, has large and luxuriant, deeply cut leaves that contrast well with other exotic foliage plants, such as paulownias and bananas (*Musa basjoo*). R. communis 'Carmencita' also looks good with metallic-blue* Eucalyptus gunnii. *It is a tender, evergreen tree-like shrub (from Africa) that needs shelter from wind as the leaves are easily damaged and hang limp once the vein along the centre is broken. We grow it as an annual, sown in April, and it achieves heights to vie with bananas if well fed and watered.*

▲ From a mid-April sowing, African marigolds (Tagetes erecta) 'Simba' are perfect for planting out in June—sown earlier, they grow too fat too soon and have to be potted on into large pots and are trickier to fit in. With dead heading, they continue to flower well into October.

▲ ▶ Zinnia 'Profusion Orange', sown at the beginning of May, is not much more than 30cm/1ft tall and effective at a border's margin.

BRIGHT FLOWERS

There is a brilliant orange African marigold, sometimes called Ragged Reggie but correctly 'Simba' (which, appropriately, means a lion). It has plenty of lacy foliage to set off the flowers but they shine right across the garden, even in mid-October. That is good with *Eupatorium capillifolium*, grown entirely for its bright green foliage, or with *Canna* 'Wyoming' (2.5m/8ft), one of the most stately with bronze foliage and orange flowers. You could fit in the inestimable and ever-popular dahlia, 'David Howard', a small apricot-orange decorative which keeps on growing through the summer and thereby hides its faded flowers so that it never needs dead-heading. You should also fit in a couple of plants of the grass *Arundo donax* var. *versicolor* in a well variegated strain where the banding of white is generously broad. The dark arum leaves of *Colocasia esculenta* 'Black Magic' are yet another suitable companion for the marigold.

You could also use, as a marigold companion, the nasturtium Jewel of Africa, which has variegated foliage, either at the front of a border or trailing and climbing, as we have it in an old brick cattle drinking tank that stands some 90cm/3ft above ground level. The nasturtium would trail over the edge of this or it could climb up anything growing in the tank that was taller than itself. We have the glaucous *Arundo donax*, cut right back each spring and growing to 3m/10ft during the summer. The dark foliage of *Canna indica* 'Purpurea' or of *C.* 'Wyoming' would also suit our purposes but we need to beware of

▼ *The small, brown-centred* Rudbeckia triloba *has powerfully yellow rays, which are smart and clean looking, adding sunshine in the Exotic Garden and to our pot displays.*

▼▼ Salvia splendens *'Rambo' is an eye-catcher in pot displays. We also grow it in the borders—as a broken trail or interspersed with blue lyme grass,* Leymus arenarius.

▶▶ *Kyle Landt in the USA sends us the seeds of* Zinnia *'Benary's Giant Lilac' every year. These giant dahlia-flowered zinnias need plenty of sunshine to give of their best—here still going strong in mid-October in the High Garden with the striped foliage and orange flowers of* Canna *'Striata' and coppery* Pennisetum setaceum *'Rubrum'.*

such partners elbowing out the protagonist, namely the 'Simba' marigold.

Zinnia Large-flowered mixed (1.2m/4ft) is a jolly mixture of all the colours and they are bold enough to earn a place in the Exotic Garden. Benary's are doing some breeding work, much of it a bit primitive, yet, but their Giant Lilac and Giant Yellow struck us in the recent zinnia trial as among the more promising. There is plenty of scope for developments, here. They would go with cannas such as 'Striata' or near a border's margin with the drooping 'tails' of *Pennisetum setaceum* 'Rubrum'.

The dwarf, small-flowered Profusion Series of zinnias is particularly pleasing in 'Profusion Orange' at a border's margin. 'Profusion White' is surprisingly satisfying. I should never have thought I should like a white zinnia.

Tithonia rotundifolia 'Torch' is an obvious zinnia relation, 1.5m/5ft tall, perhaps, and with orange flowers. You want to be a bit careful not to overfeed it, otherwise it may run to leaf at the expense of flowers. By itself, it may be short on personality, so it needs a strong supporting cast: *Canna* 'Wyoming', already described, or the variegated 'Phasion' (Tropicanna), in which the leaf is striped in surprising colours, including pink, but the flowers are orange. Dahlias go well with it too.

Salvia splendens has a well-deserved reputation for vulgarity. By and large, the breeders are responsible for this, dwarf compactness being their aim. I am sure that at the time Miss Jekyll used it in the red section of her colour-themed border, it was not an over-bred monster. The trials at Wisley are always throwing up something interesting, however, and in the case of the *S. splendens* trial it was a cultivar called 'Rambo' which, by the end of the growing season, has attained the respectable height of 90cm/3ft and has a presence. It has lost nothing of its eye-searing colour. Rather than growing it in any sort of a block, it is better to grow a broken trail of it, interspersed by something glaucous or a large agave or maybe *Colocasia esculenta* or its dark-leaved variety, 'Black Magic', or with a background of *Begonia luxurians*, which has palmate, fingered leaves. The broad-leaved grass, *Setaria palmifolia*, with parallel, longitudinal ribbing, is another possibility.

Rudbeckia brings very cheerful yellow for the later part of the season. They need good supporting foliage nearby. *R. triloba* is biennial and makes quite a large (2m/6½ft) bush in its second year, with small, brown-centred yellow daisies. There's a long list of plants you could combine it with. Same story with the striking, quite large-flowered 'Indian Summer' (1.5m/5ft), having yellow rays and a black centre. Or the rather extraordinary Cherokee Sunset Group, often not recognised as a rudbeckia by our visiting public. That is fully double in yellow, mahogany and bicolours. *Canna* 'Striata', striped yellow and green, is the perfect partner.

Celosias (common name cockscomb) are just about the most artificial-looking flowers you can imagine but they are real. Of upright habit in reds and yellows, they have a silky texture but are quite weird. Very tender. Probably not worth it, except to have people ask, 'Whatever's that?'

▶ *Spanish flag,* Ipomoea lobata, *is a stalwart with us. Sown in May, its wiry, crimson-flushed stems and stalks shin up its neighbours, here* Verbena bonariensis *and Dahlia 'Fascination'.*

▼ *Making a carpet of blossom around* Yucca gloriosa *is Petunia 'Purple Wave', each plant 90cm/3ft across by the end of the season and apparently impervious to all weathers, unlike most of its kind. The colour is only just this side of magenta and wonderfully vibrant.*

▼ ▼ *A relative newcomer with us is a flowering tobacco,* Nicotiana mutabilis, *which so far is trouble free. It grows to 1.2m/4ft and bears an airy mass of flowers that start off pure white, turn to pale pink, then age to rose pink, so you get all the colours on the plant at the same time. We sow in early May for planting out in June.*

WEAVERS AND TRAILERS

Certain petunias fit in well in the Exotic Garden. 'Purple Wave' keeps close to the ground. As is the way of petunias, it has a long season. I like to grow colchicums through it. Their season is short, but the petunias will carry on. Another type of petunia that has recently come into prominence is the Surfinia, which is treated as a perennial and vegetatively propagated. All petunias are weavers. They are good at the edge of a border but will climb into anything taller than themselves that may be behind them.

Bidens ferulifolia is a yellow daisy with a scrambling habit. Or it should have. It is better not to grow it from seed, which produces plants with an upright habit that are not good mixers. The rambling type of bidens will climb into its neighbours, as it might be the red, purple-leaved dahlia 'Bishop of Llandaff', or dahlia 'Hillcrest Royal' or the double red 'Grenadier'. Give it light and air at a path margin to start it off.

Verbena 'La France' is a long-flowering bedder that we do from cuttings. It is an excellent weaver. *Canna* 'Striata', with green and yellow striped leaves might be a good neighbour, or *Canna* 'Erebus', with narrow, glaucous leaves and abundant salmony flowers on a plant of upright habit. I'm always finding uses for that. The verbena is mauve but a good shade and I thoroughly recommend it.

Browallia americana is a small, blue-flowered infilling annual, much used in the eastern states of America but little seen here. That could be included close to a path in the Exotic Garden.

NIGHT SCENTS

Nicotiana sylvestris used to be a great favourite with us until it went down to a mildew, which hopelessly spots its fine, large leaves. If you can still grow it — and many can — you will thoroughly enjoy its bold, bright green paddle leaves and its long, tubular flowers, which droop by day but stiffen at night, when they are deliciously scented.

N. alata doesn't come into its own till evening, the flowers being limp by day. At dusk, it looks very good with orange, dark-leaved *Canna* 'Wyoming'. *N. langsdorffii* with small green flowers, is popular with many flower arrangers but it seems to me that its green flowers are swallowed up by over-dominant foliage. Red dahlias would enliven the scene.

Datura meteloides is night-flowering and fun to watch jerking itself open in the evening, but it is disappointing by and large, though it can be good in other people's gardens!

ANNUAL CLIMBERS

Always aiming at close integration of our plant material, Fergus grows masses of annual climbers to thread through just about anything that can be a host. *Mina lobata*, as we have always known it, is really *Ipomoea lobata*, a twining climber with racemes of little tubular flowers that open white and age

▲ Ipomoea tricolor 'Heavenly Blue' climbing up Solanum laxum, *a form from Brittany with lilac buds opening to white flowers. The morning glory is a thrill to discover when you first go into the garden. It loathes cold, but will romp away, sown in May, and can climb over shrubs, taking up no extra space.*

▶ *We treat purple bell vine,* Rhodochiton atrosanguineus, *as a tender biennial. It is effective draped over* Escallonia bifida *and* Eucalyptus gunnii.

to orange. We pop it into many parts of our borders to clamber up trees and shrubs and through *Verbena bonariensis*. It can do virtually what it likes, investigating neighbouring plants but without harming them. You may think it will grow in a certain direction but it will often go in another and really it hardly matters.

The annual that everyone knows as *Ipomoea tricolor* 'Heavenly Blue' is everyone's darling because pure blues are so rare and this one really is blue for a few hours after it is fully open in the morning. By midday it is changing to mauve and collapses soon after. Anything ephemeral like that is sure to touch our hearts.

That is the way it behaves in high summer. When young, the seedlings are exceedingly cold-sensitive, so we do not sow till early May. The glaucous colouring of *Eucalyptus gunnii* seedlings hosts it well. You look upwards 3m/10ft, perhaps, and there's the ipomoea, waving above all else. At shoulder level it is threading through, and giving a lift to, ageing dahlias. Once truly established, there's no stopping it right to the middle of October, at which season the flowers are much slower to die off. If the weather is dull, they will even last into the next day.

Dark flowers are easiest appreciated at close range, and so it is with *Rhodochiton atrosanguineus*, a trailing climber that takes a while to develop. It is best sown under frost-free glass the previous autumn. Both the flower calyx and the corolla are dark purple and both are showy. The corolla is a singularly dark purple tube—very striking but shed after a few days. The calyx is like a lamp-shade and persists for several weeks, which looks good when well placed in front of a lighter background. In one (unpremeditated) case, it hung in front of the broad spathe of *Canna* 'Striata', striped in yellow and green. Quite a surprise.

Thunbergia alata is a charming filler, to ramble over shrubs. It enjoys hot summers and can then make considerable growth. The flowers are rounded, expanding from a tube. Breeders have played around to vary its colouring, but I think the typical orange with a black eye is the most effective. Go somewhere like California to see it at its best.

The annual *Tropaeolum peregrinum*, known as Canary creeper, will romp away even as far north as Inverewe in Scotland, but it makes an awful lot of growth for the amount of yellow blossom. Perennial *T. speciosum* is not in my remit, but is the glory of many gardens in the north, especially when trailing over a dark yew hedge. It has rich red flowers. Its slender tubers go deep and are extremely difficult to handle. In *Tropaeolum tricolor* tubers are freely produced. This is generally best as a pot plant, flowering from March to May, with red, black and yellow in each pixie-hood flower.

Eccremocarpus scaber, the Chilean glory flower, is an annual climber with small orange/red tubular flowers. It willingly drapes itself over other plants but is itself a disappointment wherever I have seen it. A lot of growth without much to show for it. Still, it does try.

Ray Waite

COLOURFUL AND INTRICATELY MARKED FOLIAGE

Coleus (Solenostemon) *are arguably the most exciting foliage plants in general cultivation. There is an amazing range of colours and intricate markings, and Christopher loved using them for infill planting in borders and containers.*

'FROM MID AUGUST for the next two months they are making a great display,' he wrote in *Christopher Lloyd's Gardening Year*. 'Really exciting—or disgusting, according to how you view coleus.' He showed great interest in our collection at Wisley Garden.

Also known as flame nettle or painted nettle, *Solenostemon scutellarioides* is not a member of the true nettle family (*Urticaceae*) but belongs to *Labiatae* which includes such plants as mint, lavender, sage and thyme; all of which, like coleus itself, have aromatic foliage. The original introductions in the 1800s came from the Far East and, in particular, Java, where many forms were grown for decorative use. They caused a great deal of interest in gardening circles and it was not long before Victorian plant breeders set to work and produced many good cultivars. Mr F. Bause, who was employed by the Royal Horticultural Society at the garden in Chiswick, was responsible for some particularly exciting hybrids. The council of the society decided to sell by auction twelve of the best hybrids and in 1868 they were sold for £390. Coleus fever had taken hold.

As greenhouse and conservatory plants, coleus became very popular but were also used as summer

◀ *A late sowing of coleus (May) is potted on individually and brought on under cold glass at Dixter. Leaf patterns and colourings vary a lot but Fergus sorts them into groups when planting out in late July. They are still at their best in September—a Joseph's coat tapestry of colour.*

bedding subjects. They were planted on a grand scale in the sub-tropical bedding that had been perfected at Battersea Park but were not always reliable in inclement weather or cold, wet soil conditions. Even with our modern introductions, foliage colour can bleach and plant growth can be somewhat indifferent.

There are two fairly distinct types of coleus grown today: those raised from seed and the other by cuttings. The former tend to go to flower much faster than the latter and are incapable of making large specimens and certainly impossible to train into shapes. Seed-raised strains are, however, easy to propagate and the named cultivars come true to description. Even as quite small seedlings the colouring in the immature leaves gives an indication of what is to come.

SEED-SOWN COLEUS

At Great Dixter, coleus are sown in May and grown throughout in the cold frames Christopher describes on pages 170–1. Coleus, like zinnias, hate cold when in the seedling stage. If frost threatens, lengths of hessian are used to cover them. Ideally, however, coleus are sown under heated glass and the pricked-out seedlings are kept under glass, with the temperature maintained at 18 to 21°C/64 to 70°F. You can retain the spikes of blue flowers as they are not unattractive but, in my view, they spoil the effect of the foliage and also debilitate the plant. The removal of flower spikes is more important for pot-grown display specimens.

At Dixter, *Solenostemon* hybrids are grown from mixed seed and in July all the plants that 'look reasonable' are sorted by colour and markings. Some of the best available include: Wizard Group, which has a wide range of colours and makes neat plants; Rainbow Group with medium-sized leaves; 'Red Velvet' with deep-red foliage; 'Volcano' with fiery red leaves; 'Salmon Lace' with bright salmon leaves that have borders of dark red and green; and Fairway Series, which are very dwarf and produces short much-branched stems. A wide range of colours and leaf markings can be expected. The darkest-leaved cultivar is 'Palisandra' with the Kong hybrids giving the largest foliage.

CUTTINGS

The vegetatively propagated type of *Solenostemon* includes upwards of a hundred named cultivars that are available in Britain with as many more obtainable in other countries, particularly the United States of America. It is important to take care with cutting material as the indiscriminate selection of shoots can lose the character of a cultivar. Cuttings rooted in spring will produce medium-sized plants in late summer and autumn, but to grow large specimens they must be rooted in autumn and established in 9cm/3in pots. They will need careful watering in the ensuing dull months. Ideally a temperature of 10°C/50°F should be maintained but too much heat can lead to weak growth. In spring plants need to be potted on into 12cm/5in pots and subsequently into 23cm/9in or even larger containers. The strongest growing cultivars can have a diameter of well over 90cm/3ft.

Regular pinching of all the stem tips is important to keep the plants symmetrical with plenty of branches; this will need to be done at two to three week intervals. It is possible to train certain cultivars into various shapes, with standards and pyramids being the most popular. Some of the strongest growers can even be trained as fans using a framework of splayed canes. When growing these various forms, leave the leading growth(s) unpinched until the required height is reached. Standards must have their side growths removed to leave an unfurnished 'leg' except for sufficient stems at the top to develop a head which in turn will need regular pinching. Pyramids must have all their side growths left, which again must be pinched; this also applies to all the main growths as a fan is developed. Standards and pyramids must be firmly staked and ties must be inspected and if need be replaced to obviate damage to the main stems.

Cultivars worth recommendation include: 'Brightness', 'Carnival', 'Crimson Ruffles', 'Display', 'Freckles', 'Glory of Luxembourg', 'Klondike', 'Pineapple Beauty' (the last three make good standards), 'Royal Scot', 'Treales', 'Walter Turner' with 'Kiwi Fern' and 'Wisley Tapestry' having quite distinct foliage. 'Lord Falmouth' and 'Picturatus' are ideal for hanging baskets and edging for greenhouse staging.

Exotic
POT DISPLAYS
with Tom Cooper

My main use of pots is clustered on either side of the porch entrance at the front of the house, where they are a cheerful sight as I come and go. Being in a noticeable position, the plants get plenty of attention —more, probably, than those in any other part of the garden.

◀ *A late-summer pot display by the front porch with a curtain of cotoneaster providing a backdrop to a great green, fleshy* Aeonium undulatum, *furry leaved* Begonia scharffii *with blush-white flowers, red* Begonia 'Flamboyant' *and* Pelargonium 'Frank Headley' *with cream and green variegated leaves and pale salmon flowers.*

To the right of the front porch there's a *Cotoneaster horizontalis* that has been there for as long as I can remember. It's fun to have something climbing into it, such as swags of *Tropaeolum tricolor* in spring and *Ipomoea lobata* in summer. The porch is protected from our prevailing winds, except in spring, and has sunshine until mid-morning. This is perfect for begonias and doesn't seem to have an adverse effect on most of what we want to display.

We also have pot displays in the house (*Begonia scharffii*, syn. *B. haageana*, spends most of its life on the dining room windowsill), in the Wall and Sunk Gardens, on the steps leading down to the Blue Garden (don't expect any blue flowers), and in front of the shop entrance at the bottom of the garden. They can be a lot of work to keep at their best, but they are rewarding, bringing interest to areas that might otherwise be dull.

Since Fergus came to Dixter, the displays have become more and more adventurous, and more theatrical. Like Beth Chatto in her Essex garden, we use bricks or breezeblocks to set the pots at different levels. Masses of plant material is needed: architectural plants and climbers to make features at a high level, bold foliage for the middle and lower layers, as well as plenty of colour for pizzazz. We've had the ingredients to make our pots more exciting since we built greenhouses as adjuncts to the Exotic Garden (see pages 166–70). Even without shelter, if you plan ahead and have extra pots and some out-of-the-way space (as I have) for bringing along plants, you can create a succession of interest, starting with early bulbs and continuing until the frosts nip the final salvias, in November, if we're lucky. (The one I find especially irresistible is *Salvia leucantha* (90cm/3ft) with veined leaves and woolly spikes in which the calyx is rich mauve, the corolla white.)

▲ **Left**: *Daisy Lloyd with her children by the entrance porch at Dixter in September 1927. Christopher, the youngest (on the left), was six. Many years later he commandeered the Cotoneaster horizontalis to the right of the porch into service as a structure for twining plants to grow up.* **Right**: *Daisy Lloyd by the entrance porch at Dixter in 1945. Still no pot displays.*

▼&▶ *As in the Exotic Garden, our pot displays are created with structural plants forming the upper canopy, as well as the middle and lower layers. This series of photographs shows how we have been able to improve them over the years as we accumulate more exotica. Cannas,*

bananas and pseudopanax give height, begonias and aeoniums contribute substance to the middle section and cacti and succulents make excellent pot subjects low down. In between there are colourful dahlias, salvias, fuchsias and pelargoniums, as well as pretty border plants, such as heliotropes and zinnias. **Left**: *In August 1997 Canna indica 'Purpurea' at the back and Cotyledon orbiculata at the front are the strong elements but the colourful middle layer lacks an architectural component.* **Middle**: *Aeonium undulatum provides the focal point in this arrangement in July 2000, with fragrant heliotrope and arching Fuchsia 'Mr West' making a lovely show lower down.* **Right**: *Bananas and pseudopanax anchor this*

September 2006 arrangement at the back. The colours and forms of Canna indica 'Purpurea', Aeonium 'Zwartkop' and a dark-leaved sedum give substance to the middle layer, with Zinnia 'Profusion Orange' and Petunia 'Purple Wave' making a skirt of bright colour at the front. **Opposite**: *Ensete ventricosum and Pseudopanax lessonii 'Gold Splash' give height and substance to the 2005 front porch display. Begonia scharffii and dark purple and green aeoniums in the middle layer form a background to colourful Pelargonium 'Frank Headley' and fuchsias, with red salvias, yellow rudbeckias and Ipomoea lobata (scrambling over the berrying cotoneaster) jazzing up the scene beautifully.*

▲ An early June pot display includes the most spectacular of all geraniums, G. maderense, *in flower (to the left of the porch) and in leaf (on the right). Exotic banana leaves provide a backdrop to the geranium's magnificent pink flowers, as well as to aeonium alongside common-or-garden cornflowers. Yellow* Argyranthemum *'Jamaica Primrose' and blue* Heliophila longifolia *rub shoulders with* Cuphea *at the front. To the right of the porch* Tropaeolum tricolor *drapes itself over the cotoneaster.*

▶▲ *The porch two months later and we have rung the changes: plants that are over or past their peak are wheeled off stage so that cannas and dahlias can move in. The banana remains, as do the begonias—*B. scharffii *on the left and* B. luxurians *on the right next to* G. maderense, *still going strong. Grey-leaved* Celmisia semicordata *takes centre stage on the left and the* Pennisetum setaceum *'Rubrum' has moved from the wings to star on the right.*

KEEPING THE SHOW GOING

Our efforts with exotics focus on summer, when the tenders can make the most of the heat and sunshine (such as it is), but we seize every opportunity to display stimulating plants in pots. The season starts in earnest in from earliest spring with hyacinths and continues until the garden closes in October. Tulips and daffodils take over from the hyacinths and give a long season, between the different varieties. From April on, the ingredients become steadily more exotic. First to make an appearance is usually the redoubtable yellow-variegated form of *Agave americana* 'Marginata' which, surrounded by bulbs and backed with a curtain of *Tropaeolum tricolor*, acts as a harbinger of the exotica to follow. Generous sheets of sacking or fleece are kept at hand to drape over the display while nights are still cold. If a massive frost is forecast, we bring the plants inside for the night. It is still too chilly for begonias—they stay in the greenhouse until May—but aeoniums soon follow the agaves and stay put until October, as do the other good value foliage plants, which gradually come out of sheltered accommodation to act as punctuation marks: *Pseudopanax lessonii* 'Gold Splash', scheffleras, cotyledons and opuntias.

Also in April we are potting on such beauties as *Pennisetum setaceum* 'Rubrum' and *Setaria palmifolia* so they will develop into prize specimens. Nothing is put into a display until it is looking good. By early May we have hardened off *Colocasia esculenta* 'Black Magic' and are working on preparing cannas and two- to three-year-old seedlings of bananas so their really large leaves are ready to jazz up the fluffy stuff of summer.

▼ Geranium maderense *seedlings are overwintered under frost-free glass. These grow quickly, so each needs a sizeable container and to be allowed to grow into the pot before being set out in a sheltered position.*

POT ARRANGEMENTS

How to match pots and plants and how to arrange pots depends on the particular elements. A large or especially dramatic plant such as an agave or a melianthus needs space to makes its best show and ought to have a solo setting. Something smaller, an aloe or sempervivum, might do with several in one pot or several of the same plant in adjacent pots, making for a group. Different plants in the same pot (the current vogue being the more the merrier) can work, but the plants will need to have the same growing requirements. Moreover, remember that there will be a sunny and a shady side. You'll need to choose plants accordingly or rotate the container.

The not quite hardy evergreen *Geranium maderense* is extraordinary and deserves showing off in a large container. You must give it a go. It is woody (first surprise) with large, handsomely dissected leaves borne on long stalks, the whole plant making a dome about 90cm/3ft high and 1.2m/4ft across. How quickly it develops depends on how generous a treatment it receives. When it is ready, it will show its intention (as early as early February for us) through its central crown elongating. It is a multiple crown with a huge quiverful of flower buds opening over a long period. From all this effort, the leaves die off and the plant becomes hideous apart from its magenta flowers. The dying flower stalks act like guy ropes on a tent, supporting the plant as they bend back on themselves and mustn't be tidied up. You need to grow other pot plants around it to conceal its overall condition.

It is important that plant and pot be in proportion. A small plant in a large pot usually looks silly, unless you know that the plant is going to grow very

quickly, as would *Geranium maderense* or *Colocasia esculenta* 'Black Magic' (but then that has a most peculiar habit anyway). Your final effect should be of the plant dominating, not the pot. If you are using a tall pot but don't need all the soil in it, then you can fill the bottom up with hardcore (if you need the extra weight) or with polystyrene packing (if you want it light).

It's nice to have pots of all shapes and sizes. Avoid too many different shapes and sizes and, especially, a range of materials in close proximity. Rather than adding interest they invoke chaos. The whole thing can look like the dog's breakfast—what other people give their dogs, that is, since mine get nothing but the best. The shape of the pot is important, not only for showing off the plant but also for ease of getting it out of the pot. Straight-sided pots make life straightforward in this regard. Standard pots, in which height and width are the same are good for Surfinia petunias, begonias, coleus, aeoniums, agaves; long pots can be unstable but will work if wedged between other pots that will support the wobbly one.

Other things being equal, we prefer terracotta to plastic, although plastic comes in useful if the pot won't be seen. We use it for tall plants at the back

◀ Dark foliage will be almost invisible unless you can somehow highlight it. With Colocasia esculenta 'Black Magic' we use Plectranthus argentatus, a sun-loving Australian native with velvet-textured serrated leaves that in 'Hill House' are cream and green variegated. They provide a perfect foil.

◀▼ A typical Dixter summer mix in a pot display in the Mosaic Garden, with exotics rubbing shoulders with border plants. The grey leaved fan palm, Chamaerops humilis var. argentea, makes a nice, strong feature in the middle layer, with yellow rudbeckia behind it. Keeping plants in pots is a way of bringing them on and we shall keep the palm contained until it is big enough to withstand the hurly-burly of life in the ground. We use attractive terracotta containers of all shapes and sizes, especially for plants where the pot is visible. Who can tell what the pots are like for the aeoniums and dahlias towards the back of the display?

▶ Aloe saponaria in a pot display lends strength and focus to its frothy companions.

▼ What could be more exotic than the flamingo flower, Anthurium andrae-anum? The shiny heart-shaped leaves are exciting enough. Then the bright flower bracts appear, so shiny as to look lacquered, and with a protruding pale yellow, tail-like flower spadix. It's hardly surprising that they are very tricky to keep going.

of an arrangement, where the material is hidden. Plastic is cheap and light to handle and doesn't break as easily or as disastrously as terracotta. There is imitation terracotta about that looks better than plastic. It is lighter and cheaper than terracotta and can be left out all year. However, weight is sometimes an advantage.

THE ADVANTAGES OF POTS

In addition to dressing up drab spots, containers have several practical advantages. Pots are great for experimenting with plants. Anything new to us that's exotic-looking starts life in a pot—that way we can see how long it flowers, how tall it grows and how it stands up to what we can offer. We can also learn how to manage it before it takes up precious space. If it performs well at the right time, it can go into the Exotic Garden. If it doesn't come up with the goods for long enough, we can tuck the pot out of sight.

Of course, you can also tailor the soil, the fertilizer, and the water exactly to the needs of demanding plants, and you can move the containers about to make sure the plants are getting just the conditions they need.

Pots can also be shifted onstage or off depending on their state. *Beschorneria yuccoides* belongs to *Agavaceae* and produces a sizable rosette of broad glaucous leaves resembling a yucca (of course). It is hardy only in such maritime spots as the Isle of Wight, the Devon and Cornish coasts. For most of us it needs protection. The tubular flowers are green and pink, borne on long, arching, pink stalks. This is quite an extraordinary sight. Flowering in May, I should not call it a useful garden ingredient, although it is widely offered. Much better to keep it in a container, whisking it on display in earliest spring and then clearing it away when the flowering is finished. The plant is monocarpic, so the crown dies after flowering, but new pups are always produced, so your supply will increase.

With plants like bananas, which cannot be easily or inexpensively bought in large sizes, carrying them over the winter in their container in a glasshouse or cool room allows you to bulk them up and make a bigger presence in the garden. In colder parts of the USA gardeners do this with cannas as well as with bananas and other large-scale tenders. Sinking the containers directly into open spots in the border gives a garden a slightly tropical air, often catching visitors off guard.

▼ A straight-sided pot made by Alan Caiger-Smith and planted by Tara Cully with opuntias, echeveria and Cotyledon orbiculata.

▲▲ *A pot display in the Blue Garden with pelargonium, begonias and rudbeckia in good-looking shallow terracotta pots, and Pennisetum setaceum 'Rubrum' and golden-leaved Agastache rugosa 'Golden Jubilee' in larger pots. Behind are some of our favourite dahlias —orange 'David Howard', magenta 'Hillcrest Royal' and crimson 'Chimborazo', with an aeonium to lend some gravitas to the scene.*

▲ *We use bold, architectural plants as punctuation marks in our pot displays. Here, the large leaves of a banana jazz up the fluffy stuff: fuchsias, begonias and the lacy foliage of silvery white Centaurea cineraria.*

▶▶ *Tara Cully watering the pots by the porch on a misty morning in late September. Giving each plant what it needs is a job that requires precision and judgement —some need water and some don't.*

POT PRACTICALITIES

Drainage holes in containers are of the greatest importance. There must be plenty of them and they must be crocked. That is to say that over each hole a concave piece of crock—a broken chip of earthenware or plastic—is placed, hollow side down, to allow the free passage of water. No need for a thick layer of crockery as people once insisted, just make sure the hole can't be blocked and the soil can't escape.

What you put in the pot for soil must depend on the plant. For most pots, we use John Innes No 2 and for shrubby plants the stronger No 3, both of which are loam-based. They are easy to water and to wet again. They also are heavy, so they provide stability for the containers. You can adjust the mix to suit your needs—adding extra composted bark for a fern, or grit for extra drainage for a succulent. When potting, leave a good space at the top to allow for generous watering without needing to do the job twice, almost immediately. Make sure your compost is level in the pot, as this enables even watering. See that the pots themselves are level. Fine gravel below them makes this easy.

We feed our pots with Phostrogen twice a week later in the season (after the goodness in the compost has been used up). On older specimens we apply a dressing of 3-months or 6-months Osmocote or some other slow-release fertilizer early in the season. You are asking plants in pots to perform hard, so you must feed them well (and also the regular watering washes away some of the fertilizer).

WATERING CONTAINERS

This is the trickiest operation to get right. Water sparingly until the plants are growing strongly. Different plants have different needs. Watering should be done when the plant needs it and not automatically. This can be every day or even twice a day if the weather is very hot and the pot is in an exposed position. It is best done in the morning, when transpiration is not too rapid. For the same reason, avoid watering at midday. Don't assume that because it rained during the night, you are off the hook. More likely that's not the case. Dew can be deceptive, too. Tap the pot. A dull, thudding response indicates the presence of plentiful moisture. Lift the pot and judge from its weight. If still in doubt, water it. Don't splash the water all over the place. Be precise and be thorough. This is where a long-spouted Haws watering can is so useful. The water can be aimed at the exact spot where it is needed. You will know you have thoroughly watered the pot when water begins to escape from the drainage hole at the bottom.

Don't fall into a trance while you are watering your pots. A succulent aeonium, with small water requirements, may be next to a fuchsia, which rapidly gets thirsty. After watering a plant, dead-head and weed it. The hairy bittercress (*Cardamine hirsuta*), known as jumping Jesus, for instance, is always sneaking into pots.

Tim Miles

EDIBLE EXOTICS IN POTS

In our minds' eye the quintessential exotic garden would be similar to our vision of Eden — lush vegetation with an abundance of flamboyant blooms and a proliferation of succulent fruit.

POT-GROWN MATERIAL is an important part of many exotic gardens whether on a largish scale as we have at The Cotswold Wildlife Park or in a small back yard, veranda or terrace. As in any other type of planting, it is beneficial to contrast not only colour, but also the texture and form of plants. In exotic gardens this is achieved mostly with foliage, with the three basic textures being bold, as in banana, fine as in *Cyperus papyrus* and tree fern and spiky as in *Phormium* and *Yucca*. The use of fine textured plants is crucial in giving a sense of the vast scale of the likes of banana leaves — without that reference point a bunch of big-leaved plants would be far less effective. At Great Dixter drifts of *Verbena bonariensis* help to achieve this.

BANANAS

Bananas are the most dramatic of all the exotics we can grow in a temperate climate and they can be very successful in pots if their thirst and hunger are satisfied. They have strong root systems and appreciate being regularly 'potted on'. At The Cotswold Wildlife Park, we use a combination of drip irrigation and simple automatic timers so that water is applied regularly and efficiently. Water retentive gels can help by reducing the frequency of watering but generally should not be relied upon. A generous dose of controlled release fertilizers will encourage continued growth well into autumn although, as with most

exotics, try to avoid soft growth at the end of the season which can result in die-back and fungal problems. High potash feeds are useful at this stage in order to toughen up new growth.

The hardier species such as *Musa basjoo* (Japanese banana) can have their stems cut to the ground by hard frosts, so we wrap them, as Fergus does, to ensure a more imposing display the following summer. *M. sikkimensis* is slightly less hardy but irresistible in forms such as 'Red Tiger' which has striking leaf markings. Smaller-growing still is the densely clumping *Musella* which is particularly well suited to pot culture. If you want bananas to eat then consider the tough but tasty *Musa* × *paradisiaca* 'Dwarf Orinoco'. Remember that the roots of pot-grown specimens are more susceptible to the frost so keep them protected during the coldest months.

The tender *Ensete ventricosum* is virtually essential to the jungle look and is particularly effective when back-lit by low evening or rich autumn sunlight. It is seed raised and very rapid — eighteen months from sowing you can have a monster on your hands. Of its purple forms, *E. v.* 'Montbeliardii' is more vertically inclined, elegant and of stronger constitution than *E. v.* 'Maurelii'. These plants are not the easiest to lift and containerize if bedded out for the summer, so we grow them permanently in a container. With huge leaves that catch the wind like sails, their stability is a concern, so we use wide-based pots, a loam-based compost and metal stabilizing frames.

FRUIT-BEARERS

There are plenty of other exotic-looking plants that bear fruit and do well in pots. Citrus, which have long been cultivated in pots in temperate northern climes (think of the orangeries at gardens such as Dunham Massey in Cheshire and Hestercombe in Somerset), actually prefer to be out of doors for as much of the season as possible. Most will be undamaged by light frost, other than on soft spring growth. I rate the cultivar *Citrus* × *meyeri* 'Meyer', as it is compact, more cold tolerant than most, and seldom without scented flowers and fruit. Give it an acidic loam-based compost and regular use of a designer citrus feed.

Fresh figs from your own garden are difficult to surpass. Growing them in pots restricts the root run, thus reducing their vigour and encouraging fruiting. It also enables them to be moved to frost-free quarters to protect the overwintering embryo fruit, which will then mature the following summer. Some varieties, such as 'Brown Turkey', are more reliable fruiters in Britain, while others, such as 'Cambridge Builder', have particularly luxuriant foliage.

The grey-green leaves of olives provide classic Mediterranean imagery. They are available in a wide range of sizes, including gnarled specimens of some age transplanted from redundant groves, which can make a perfect centrepiece for a Mediterranean style garden. Old vineyard plants can also be obtained, but don't expect too much palatable fruit in our climate with these varieties. Some, however, do offer a reasonable quality of edible fruit in cooler conditions — 'Regent' has been good with us in a hottish spot.

In our 'Eden' there must be an Apple! For a pot I would choose 'Red Devil' or 'Red Falstaff' on a dwarfing or semi-dwarfing rootstock. Both are durable, trouble-free and self fertile, bearing late hanging bright red fruit. The latter has large and frost-resistant blossoms.

There are also dwarf or smaller growing types of peach, nectarine (guard against 'leaf curl' with these two) and apricot which fruit in summer, and are recommended for pot culture. Guava, pineapple guava, sharon fruit (*Diospyros kaki* 'Fuyu') are other exotic possibilities.

CLIMBERS AND SCRAMBLERS

These naturally rely on other plants for physical support, their less substantial roots being designed more for gaining sustenance than strong anchorage. This helps make them good long-term candidates for pot culture. The kiwi fruit (*Actinidia deliciosa*) is an impressive foliage vine. Its self-fertile variety 'Jenny' requires no mate to set a respectable crop of smallish tasty fruit. Passion fruit (*Passiflora caerulea*) can provide a mass of bright yellow fruit, of no culinary consequence, which hang for some weeks. It sometimes needs a pollinating partner but there are self fertile forms. More tender types such as *P.* 'Amethyst' are worth experimenting with in warm corners.

With large leaves, far reaching tentacles and rampant habit, pumpkins and other cucurbits can provide a jungle feel, with the bizarre-shaped fruit of some climbing gourds adding to the fun. Consider, too, other subjects traditionally of the kitchen garden. The runner bean, for instance, was originally introduced to Europe as a flowering ornamental and there are now white- as well as scarlet- or red-flowered varieties available, and climbing beans with strikingly coloured pods, such as 'Empress'. Consider too *Lablab purpureus* 'Ruby Moon' which provides a triple-whammy of attractive foliage, flower and pods.

◀ *Christopher was a self-styled 'fig pig', and almost as fond of the leaves as of the luscious fruit. As he wrote of the foliage in Gardener Cook, 'it is small wonder that Adam adopted it when obliged to cover his genitals. How he managed between October and May, history does not relate.'*

PRACTICAL
MATTERS

We garden intensively. Nowhere more so than in the Exotic Garden. The work here is concentrated around, though not confined to, two periods in the year: planting time, which should have got under way by the beginning of June, and lifting time in the autumn.

During the growing season there are the usual routine jobs of weeding, deadheading and supplementary staking. In addition, as you might expect where leaves are large and growth prodigious, there is a certain amount of peacekeeping between quarrelling neighbours, and rescuing of the overwhelmed. In the dormant season work is confined to sporadic checks on the sleeping beauties.

SPRING PREPARATIONS

Growth begins before we are ready for it. The warmth of spring has its effect in the greenhouses and frames, and the activity of the plants forces us, in turn, to some kind of activity. But what? There may be short-sleeved days in March, but we might yet be tobogganing in April and still clutching our clouts in early May. A rash move is certain to invite disaster, yet there is still plenty to get on with. Dahlias and cannas must be brought into the light and, if possible, heat. Cuttings will be taken from the shooting dahlias, while the cannas are divided and repotted. Seed, of some kind, will need to be sown almost every week well into May.

The greenhouses need careful supervision at this time of year. Plants which have benefited from being on the dry side all winter are suffering on the same account. Bouts of mild weather are an opportunity to give desiccated pots a good soak and a liquid feed. Increased watering will mean increased humidity and subsequent rot and fungi. Maximum ventilation must be provided at every opportunity, without forgetting to shut all down again by

◀ Agave americana 'Marginata' in the wheelbarrow and ready to start its journey to the potting shed to be prepared for overwintering in a cold frame (see pages 170–1). Some plants are large and awkward to lift and house, but when this handsome beast comes out in April, the trouble seems worthwhile. It performs right the way through to the first frosts.

The greenhouses need careful supervision during the months before planting time. We prop the door open, by day, whenever the weather is mild and the wind not howling through. We also give pots a good soak and a liquid feed, and generally make sure they are in good shape. Peeling off dead foliage and top dressing with fresh potting compost may be enough, but some plants will want re-potting.

▶ In late May, the Exotic Garden has been ready for several weeks, with the beds weeded and plenty of goodness added to the soil. The phormiums (here P. 'Sundowner' in Bed 4) have been tidied, stooled Eucalyptus gunnii are covered in healthy young foliage and Tetrapanax papyrifer is ready to expand to jungle proportions. We are waiting for the weather and our energy levels to be just right for several days' concentrated effort.

nightfall. Leaves expand and everything has constantly to be rearranged and moved from one spot to another. By planting time it is a relief to be able to get the things into the ground and leave them to their own devices.

Meanwhile, the ground itself will need some attention. We leave the exotic garden clear and fallow in the off season. It is an enclosed and separate space so we can get away with that. All the same, it will need digging over, weeding and feeding. The permanent ingredients have to be spruced up. The paulownias and the eucalypts are stooled; the yuccas and the phormiums tidied; *Acer negundo* 'Flamingo' and the aboriginal roses pruned. Self-sowers are thinned, mercilessly (they can easily dominate, as *Verbena bonariensis* was inclined to, some years ago), and superfluous suckers are removed from *Tetrapanax papyrifer* and *Rhus* × *pulvinata,* and potted up for sale in the nursery. Once we are moderately certain that the danger of frost is past (emergency measures can always be taken if we are proved wrong) the protected permanent ingredients, most obviously the bananas, can be unwrapped. They will look odd and anaemic for a day or two, but it is amazing what a bit of fresh air will do for them.

▶ *Cannas and dahlias lined up in the shade of the hovel are ready for planting out on a perfect morning in early June. This is a good time to split the canna rhizomes, if you want to increase your stock. Be warned that the young shoots are brittle and horribly easy to snap off. Between the posts of the hovel can be seen some of the permanent planting in Bed 7:* Trachycarpus fortunei *and the massive stem of* Escallonia bifida.

▼ *Bed 10 ready for planting, the self-seeding corn marigold and verbena yet to be thinned. Plenty of foliage variety is provided by the permanent ingredients, yucca, eucalypts, tetrapanax, ferns and* Rosa *'Mrs Oakley Fisher', which has purple young foliage and single, apricot-coloured flowers. Christopher wrote that he grew this rose 'out of sentiment as much as for the rose itself. My plant came from a cutting given to me by Vita Sackville-West. Roses are often exceedingly long-lived and this one must be fifty years old.'*

The grand planting at the start of June is quite an event. We usually start at 5 a.m. That's the hour I get up anyway in the summer to turn on the sprinklers and, having savoured the dawn, usually go back to bed for an hour. Early morning is very precious. All is quiet and fresh and seems to close the garden intimately around me, so that when I speak, to one of the dogs, it is as though we were in the privacy of a well-furnished room.

Timing is vital. We have been waiting for the weather and our energy levels to be just right for several days' concentrated effort. With an early start, we can get a lot of plants into position before the sun is overhead. I say 'we' do the planting, but these days it's Fergus on his knees in the borders, with me as 'co-director of operations'.

The pots are set out in the shade, looked at, considered, turned and moved and reconsidered, bearing in mind each plant's eventual potential. Also its, and its neighbour's, requirements. More plants are called for. 'Isn't there a better specimen of that somewhere in the frames?' The succulents look thin, the begonias weedy, the setarias as though they should be on life-support. But we have done this before and know what it will be like in not many weeks, when those spiky canna snouts have become great leaves slapping at our faces, engulfing us in pleasure.

▶ Fergus's sketch for Bed 10, showing how we plan sweeps of dahlias and cannas in the spaces, although all may change when planting gets going. Fergus explains: 'Spaces between our structural plants help us think more clearly. You don't want anything to restrict your creativity.'

Xanthophthalmum segetum

Verbena bonariensis

Fuchsia 'Mr West'

Fuchsia 'Lena'

Farfugium japonicum 'Argenteum'

Yucca gloriosa

Dicksonia squarrosa

Canna 'Musifolia'

Dahlia 'Grenadier'

Eucalyptus gunnii

Tetrapanax papyrifer

Melianthus major

Eucalyptus gunnii

Rosa 'Mrs Oakley Fisher'

Thalia dealbata

Choice of material for each bed—some are sunnier than others, for instance—has been under discussion for months and orders have been made to augment our stock. Fergus will have sketched a plan for each bed similar to the one on page 147. It changes every year.

Once you get to know your plants and your site you can be exact about what should go where. You can also become more adventurous. Experiments based on prior knowledge are the least likely to go wrong. That said, there will always be surprises, and you should be prepared to judge the surprises on their merits. Weather has its influence. One year the dahlias will be shy, but at their best at the end of October; another time they'll flourish and spend themselves in August. There must be something else to look at. The picture should be complex without being full of complications.

◀ *How to arrange our planting of dahlias, cannas and exotica that have overwintered under heated glass involves discussion every step of the way. We change the original plans as each bed is filled, making adjustments as the plants go in.*

▼ From far left:

• The dogs, Canna and Yucca, enjoy being part of the operation. Each plant gets a big dose of water. We have an old bodge, filled from a hose with water, into which the watering cans are dipped as required. The debris that piles up is cleared away as each bed is completed.

• Spacing is vital if the plants are to make the jungly effect we are after. Here dahlias are planted 45cm/18in apart.

• Fergus thins Verbena bonariensis so as to leave just enough to create a connecting thread through the garden. Removing a few thousand self-sown seedlings each year, for the sake of the few we leave, is an effort, but worthwhile.

• The verbena has been thinned, leaving room on the corner for Tetrapanax papyrifer and Melianthus major to expand and, once the canopy has lifted, we'll be able to tuck a begonia beneath.

Staking is something that must be considered, now and later. Dahlias, in particular, are absolutely reliant on bamboo support. We allow one stout cane per plant, and involve all the stems in an interdependency with tarred twine and clove hitches. The principle is that the system must be invisible and invincible. A plant that looks trussed and oven-ready is worse than a flopping, half-broken wretch. Neither is excusable. The stake must be sufficient to deal with the plant's eventual height and weight, and a close eye kept during the following weeks so that more string will be added as the plant burgeons skywards.

We rely on shade lovers, like begonias, to colonize the spaces beneath taller plants. The timing here can be tricky, with a certain amount of scorching being inevitable while things settle in and before the leaves of the overarching plant have expanded. Where the shade-lover is particularly delicate, precious or in some other way capable of exciting our pity to the point of action, temporary shade can be provided. A couple of canes and a bit of hessian or burlap will do the trick.

The paths having been swept and the black pots banished, the Exotic Garden is set for the season. It must be irrigated, but otherwise it can be left to plump up for a week or two. At this time of year you turn your back for a moment and the gaps have vanished, and where there was bare ground and a copse of stakes, there are walls of greenery about to burst into colour.

◀ *Staking dahlias needs to be done in good time, that is before plants collapse and never look the same again, and it must be effective yet unobtrusive.*

From top left:

- *Set the cane behind the plant and hammer it in, making sure it is the right way up and vertical (they look appalling with the thicker end pointing up and leaning this way and that).*
- *Hammer in the cane until it is rock steady. On hard ground we make a preliminary hole with a metal peg.*
- *Trim the cane to the correct length, that is, long enough to support the growing flower stem but not so long as to stick up.*

- *More stems, more canes. Use enough, but not too many.*
- *Make a clove hitch in a length of unobtrusive green string.*

- *Place the clove hitch over the cane.*
- *Loop the string round the dahlia's stem, taking the end…*
- *…on to the next cane.*

SUMMER MAINTENANCE INTO AUTUMN

The Exotic Garden is kept fresh and vital throughout its season. We expect it to keep its head up, right until the last minute when it is taken apart again for the winter. Assiduous dead-heading is vital. Ideally, this should be done daily, as with the picking of sweet peas. Essentially, it must be done by someone who knows not to leave a trail of snags behind them. Flower and stem must be taken away cleanly, down to the next bud. As the season progresses, the cannas will need dead-heading, as well as the dahlias.

As the taller ingredients approach their potential, gaps, inevitably, appear at their feet. We are ready for this. Begonias, impatiens and farfugiums are waiting in the wings to be slotted in wherever gaps appear. These shade lovers are essential in providing a lower story in the overall picture.

Gaps also appear where we've been pulling out corn marigolds. At the beginning of the season, these self-sowers provide a splash of sunshine, but there comes a point when they are about to be scraggy. They have to go. Meanwhile we have been planting morning glories and the very different, but closely related, *Mina* (actually *Ipomoea*) *lobata*. If these are set out too soon the leaves are apt to turn yellow on a cold night, to the detriment of the whole plant. In any case they are to come into their own much later in the season. The morning glories will thread through, and give a lift to, the ageing dahlias, while the mina will clamber through *Verbena bonariensis* which will, by then, have the strength to carry it.

Where big leaves, such as those of the tetrapanax, hang out over a path that is in constant use they quickly become tattered. Loath though Fergus is to do it, it is better to remove them and let the plant devote its energies to making other leaves in more sensible places. The editing of big leaves, in general, is a constant topic as we go through the Exotic Garden.

▶ *Daily dead-heading is vital, the cut on a dahlia needing to be made right back to where the stem branches and the next flower bud is located. If done sloppily, so that snags are left behind, it sets your teeth on edge—or should do. With cannas, it's just a matter of tugging at the gaudy bunch of satiny flowers.*

▶▶ *Rapid growth requires generous feeding and watering. We are lucky enough to have our own water supply and to be able to have irrigation blitzes. There's no point in just giving a sprinkle as you pass. To be effective, the water needs to be continuous and for a couple of hours so it reaches the plants' lowest roots. And it is best done early in the morning or at the end of the day.*

◀ It's the beginning of November—morning glory is still producing flowers every day and dahlias make it a wonderful time to be in the garden. And such a feast for all the insects that we like to see: 'To set budding more and still more later flowers for the bees, Until they think warm days will never cease', as Keats wrote. However, Dahlia 'Hillcrest Royal' is beginning to flag and will be lifted as soon as frost has blackened the foliage.

▲ Almost back to basics, this is Bed 4 after we have removed the plants that would be killed outright by frost. Fergus works off planks, especially after rain, to avoid compacting the soil.

AUTUMN GLORIES

Tender plants have no idea what is about to hit them. All through September and much of October, despite the hints of shortening days and cooling nights that warn our hardy natives to duck and cover, they go on stretching into the autumn sunshine, oblivious to their potential doom. Luckily for them, we are there to come to the rescue.

You may need nerves of steel to cut down and dig up a plant just as it is reaching the peak of its glory. If the summer was cool then some of the salvias may not have got to their full flowering potential until the middle of September. The opuntias will be at their fattest and the aeoniums at their headiest. A dahlia like 'Grenadier' might be long past its peak, but the elusive 'Admiral Rawlings' could well have only begun to flower in double figures. All this has to be ignored. You know what the plants don't know: that devastation is on its way; there might be a bit of global warming about but we're a long way from a frost-free winter yet.

▲ The same *Agave americana* 'Marginata' as on page 142, about to leave the Exotic Garden to spend winter in a cold frame.

▼ In the potting shed, Einav Gabriel tidies the agave and gives it fresh compost.

PREPARATIONS FOR WINTER

We need to be organised. When you want to take plants under cover, make sure that everything is ready and prepared to receive them so that they are not kept hanging around. Well ahead of time, make sure that you have enough pots and of the right sizes. It is all too easy to have masses of small pots and not enough of the larger sizes. Clean pots are best. Prepare or buy compost. We actually mix our own, using the John Innes, soil-based formula. According to what it is to be used for, we then adjust it.

For begonias we add composted bark to make the mixture more open. For succulents we add 6mm/¼in crushed horticultural grit to the mix, up to 50 per cent, depending on the requirements of the plant. Cacti like an almost vertical drainage, while aeoniums only need the compost to be opened up a little. We also prepare a cuttings compost for begonias and succulents. There is a huge range of composts on the market, tailored to every need, and you could easily buy one of these. Trial and error, however, will inevitably lead to some adjustment in whatever compost you buy (and how many different bags can you fit under your bench anyway?). There is something to be said for finding a couple of good base composts, one John Innes and one soil-less. By mixing them together or not, and adding grit in varying proportions, you will cover most of the formulae you require.

▶ *Lifting the newly potted agave is a two-person job — Fergus in the cold frame, Matt Reese taking half the weight from the outside.*

▼ *Agave americana 'Marginata' in the cold frame, where it will stay, covered by a light, from November to April, until a warm spring day prompts us to bring it out of storage so as to acclimatize before planting in the Exotic Garden in June.*

THE LIFTING PROCESS

There is an order of priority when we come to taking plants out of the ground. First to come in are the begonias, succulents and anything that would be killed outright by frost, like *Euphorbia cotinifolia.* We listen anxiously to the frost forecasts, especially at the weekends when the worst tends to happen. Other plants in this category are *Cyperus papyrus* (the Egyptian papyrus); *Pennisetum setaceum* 'Rubrum'; *Setaria palmifolia,* a glamorous grass that always looks at death's door by the spring but recovers dramatically; *Trevesia palmata,* normally treated as a house plant anyway; and *Colocasia esculenta* 'Black Magic', a plant that tends to be more than half in love with easeful death. Plants in this category, apart from the succulents, are brought into a hot house, to be kick-started into new growth. This gives them a greater chance of overcoming the injury of their disinterment.

Prickly cacti need to be handled with respect. Wear gloves and use a plastic compost bag slit down the sides as a kind of sling. Pieces, inevitably, will drop off, particularly with the opuntias. These can be saved and used as cuttings material the following spring. Out of the ground, succulents become very top heavy, so you need to support them constantly while you work. You also need to watch your back, as you are handling something awkward and heavy, with some tricky manoeuvring thrown in and, possibly, a bit of fancy footwork when you dodge the surrounding plants and carelessly abandoned tools. Take your time. A very gritty compost, aside from providing good drainage, will help to lower the plant's centre of gravity once it is potted. It is also less inclined to leave air holes around the root ball, so there is no need to give the plant a detrimental soaking (apart from the aeoniums, which would probably appreciate a good water). Give the pot a bang and a shake instead, to

▶ *The tropical aroid,* Colocasia esculenta, *is the sort of plant you want to look at several times a day to see what its great heart-leaves are up to. But now, at the beginning of November, enough people have swished by for a season and it is beginning to look past its prime.*

▶▶ From top left:

- *In preparation for lifting the colocasia, Fergus cuts off the top growth to about 30cm/1ft.*
- *He digs up the plants, taking care not to spike the tubers with the fork, separates them and shakes off excess soil as he goes.*
- *Two clumps have yielded seven plants, all with healthy roots.*

- *Some gardeners let the tubers dry out and store them as dahlias, but we find we get bigger and better plants if we pot them up in soil-based compost.*
- *The potted colocasias on their way to the greenhouse.*

- *Under the greenhouse bench, the colocasias get minimal light but more than they would in the cellar. After spending the winter in a frost-free place, we start them up again under warm, close conditions the next spring.*

settle the compost. Make sure, as you put the pot away, that each plant is steady and not going to topple the minute your back is turned.

With the other plants, shake excess soil off the root ball. Prune the top if there has been much root loss, the one compensating for the other. Take cuttings from the tops in any case. Pot into a comfortable sized pot, leaving some space on the outside, but not too much. Eliminate all air pockets. You can use a wooden label for this. Water, and place in the greenhouse.

Rather than hang on to an old plant, it is sometimes better to throw it away and start again with young stock from cuttings. Large plants like *Pseudopanax* and *Cyperus papyrus* can be difficult to house. Young stock is often a better choice, otherwise you have to either prune hard or risk leaving them outside. The *Cyperus* hates being disturbed in the autumn. If you must, put it straight into your warmest house in a tub of water. The high heat will kick it back into growth (you hope).

The *Pennisetum* and the *Setaria*, being other potential invalids, are cut hard back to reduce leaf area and stimulate new growth. It isn't easy. Always keep by you a few young but already established plants to fall back on, in case of accidents or failures. Having known no better life than that in a pot, they are more likely to tolerate it for the winter and be ready for a kick-start into growth in the spring.

◀ *Lifting cacti and succulents for over-wintering can be a prickly business. Fergus uses newspaper to hold an opuntia while lifting it with the fork.*

▼ From below top left:

- *Lifting the opuntia and shaking off excess soil.*
- *Carefully laying the opuntia in the wheelbarrow.*
- *Lifting Cotyledon orbiculata.*

- *A wheelbarrowful of cacti and succulents.*
- *Fergus's journey from the Lutyens steps takes him past Gunnera manicata growing on the edge of the lower moat.*
- *Potting the opuntia into a large terracotta pot, using gritty, well-drained compost.*
- *Fergus ducks low as he takes the newly potted opuntia out of the potting shed.*

▶ *The opuntia joins its fellow succulents in the greenhouse. The roof lights can be left open during the day until frost threatens.*

▼ *Lifting dahlias for winter storage:
Removing top growth; Digging up, taking
care to get the spade deep beneath the
tubers so as to avoid damaging them;
Removing old soil; Potting up the tubers
in old potting compost; Labelling the pot.*

▶ Top: *Dahlias and cannas lined up
in pots and plastic crates in the cellar.*
Below: *We swaddle* Musa basjoo *in a
thick padding of bracken and other fern
fronds. It periodically tries to break out
of this, but we refuse to release it till the
following June.*

TOUGHER CUSTOMERS

Some plants can be allowed to be frosted before taking action on their behalf. Dahlias and cannas are stored as tubers and rhizomes respectively, so they can be left until frost has blackened the foliage. They are then lifted and stored in boxes of compost somewhere cool but frost-free. Cellars, in our case. They need to be checked regularly as shrivelling will result if the compost is allowed to dry completely. So, now and again, through the winter, they are visited and given a watering to ensure they remain plump. Not everyone has a cellar, I know, and those that have might use it for other purposes, but a frost-free shed or a shelf in the garage will do.

THE PROTECTION RACKET

The list of plants that can remain outside, given a bit of protection, seems to be growing every year. Not so much as a result of the climate, but as our acquaintance with each plant deepens and we begin to understand its true nature. The small tree fern *Dicksonia squarrosa*, for instance, has a wooden framed box, open on one side and otherwise covered with bubble plastic, which we drop over it when it gets cold. *Beschorneria yuccoides* has horticultural fleece draped over it. *Musa basjoo* is given a thick wrapping of dead fern fronds, through which young leaves will poke, sometimes as early as February. Some, such as *Tetrapanax papyrifer*, used to spend the winter cosseted in the greenhouse, until we discovered that the roots that were left in the ground, unprotected, formed a new colony of their own the following year. We still lift a couple of pieces for insurance, but have yet had to resort to them. Yet other plants are lined up outside, out of the wind, to see how they will survive the winter — agaves and cordylines, for example.

We have four greenhouses (there was only one when Fergus came to me), all made of cedar with a brick or concrete block base. They are relatively small in size and look in keeping with their surroundings.

The oldest is our coldest (kept frost-free with a little heater that switches on when a frost is forecast). This house is well ventilated with all the windows kept open as much as possible and is packed with cuttings. These are mostly rooted, but the last thing we want in autumn, is to have to pot them individually, thereby taking up far more space and becoming ready for sale long before they can be housed in a cold frame and long before the customer is ready to look after them. They get and look starved, but will soon come round in spring, when we can pot them individually and house them in cold frames. The sun is then strong enough to look after them by day. At night, if necessary, we can cover them with hessian, or some-such, removing it when the outside air warms up. If it remains frosty day and night, the frames will remain covered throughout. Total darkness will do no harm under those conditions, apart from grey mould (botrytis) fungus taking over. Given that danger, we may need to open up and spray with fungicide. On the whole, we would aim to keep the atmosphere dry. Fuchsias, geraniums, *Salvia involucrata*, *Helichrysum petiolare*, *Artemisia arborescens*, *Plectranthus argentatus* and *Amicia zygomeris* are kept here as cuttings. *Tropaeolum tricolor* and *Gladiolus tristis* are kept as pot plants in this cool but frost-free environment.

We have a second frost-free house for cacti and succulents. These are kept ticking over, relatively dry and require little attention. Some, like the agaves and aeoniums, are kept in large pots, and others, like the succulent senecios, cotyledons and echeverias, are stored as cuttings to be potted up to grow on in the spring before planting out in the summer. This house is left well ventilated only to be closed up, and the heater turned on, during frosty nights.

The third, a sunk greenhouse, is maintained at a minimum temperature of 3–4°C/37–39°F. The pit is an old and effective device to retain warmth. Our houses are exposed to a lot of wind, which cools them down, even though it is from the southwest. This house has daturas, bananas, tibouchinas, as well as the hardier begonias in it. There is also a heated bench and a mist unit for propagation here. This house is ventilated every day for short periods and during milder spells will have the vents open for most of the day. During cold weather the house is kept shut, but good air movement is ensured by switching the ventilation fan on.

The begonia house, which contains a lot more besides, is the hottest, the temperature not allowed to drop below 10°C/50°F by means of an electric fan heater with a thermostat. The vents are opened only in the mildest weather during winter but care needs to be taken as begonias hate cold drafts. Good air movement is ensured by switching on the fan on a regular basis. *Cyperus papyrus*, *Pennisetum setaceum* 'Rubrum', *Setaria palmifolia*, *Colocasia esculenta* 'Black Magic' and *Euphorbia cotinifolia* are all in this house.

▼ *Tender* Cyperus papyrus *and* Colocasia esculenta *'Black Magic' in the begonia house where the temperature is not allowed to drop below 10°C/50°F by means of an electric fan heater with a thermostat, which also ensures good air movement.*

▲ Cacti and succulents are kept ticking over and relatively dry in our second greenhouse. It has a strong framework of staging with a lip wide enough to take a layer of corrugated iron sheets, laid so as to allow excess water to pass through, topped with 5mm/³⁄₁₆in grit or gravel, which is coarse enough to drain well but fine enough to stand pots level on it. We spread another layer of fine gravel on the earth underneath the staging.

▶▶ Begonias overwintering in the begonia house. If you pot them up into fresh compost in spring, when the weather warms up and light intensity increases, you will get the largest and most glamorous leaves.

CHOOSING A GREENHOUSE

Your greenhouse can be anything from a distinctly home-made affair of recycled timber and clear plastic to a state-of-the-art automated plant palace with period details. In between there are a multiplicity of choices to be made. Should you have wood or metal for instance? Wood has better heat retention, and these days, if cedar isn't affordable, can be treated to be reasonably durable. Aluminium can be cheap, and requires less maintenance though, because it radiates heat, it has a drying effect and will cost you more in heating. The cheapest grades are flimsy.

Our next question is do we use glass or polycarbonate sheeting for glazing. Glass looks better — always has. It develops less algal growth and is less liable to 'popping out' (this happens as the sheet buckles and comes loose of its frame). Standard horticultural glass is 3mm/⅛in thick, it's cheap but it can be weak and dangerous when smashed. Toughened glass is the safer option but this is a lot more expensive.

Polycarbonate sheeting can be used for greenhouses, cold frames, con- servatories and roof lights. Thickness varies and the greater the thickness, the better the insulation, but the worse the light transmission. It is easy to use (to cut and fix down), and is safe and insulates well. It is made up of two sheets joined together with a gap between them. It is tough, damage-resistant and yet flexible. Being insulated, it is good on energy saving. When ultra-violet light-stabilized, it has a longer life and less discolouration. These sheets are lightweight, easy to transport and to install. Large sheets can make installing easy. You can also buy bronze-coloured sheets, which reduce sun glare.

Make sure the site of your greenhouse is light. Avoid shade, as you can always provide this where you need it. Choose a sheltered spot that doesn't flood. Position the house to run east–west, for maximum light, which is

especially important in winter. If your house is a lean-to, paint the back wall white for increased light reflection. Avoid frost pockets. Think about the availability of water and electricity to your greenhouse. A thermometer is vital. You can have a radio-remote one now, so that you can check the temperature in your greenhouse without leaving your fireside (it won't tell you whether the plants are alive).

Ventilation is vitally important, but provision for it is always inadequate. The greater the means you have to ventilate, the better your control. Ideally, the equivalent of one fifth of the total floor area should be devoted to ventilation. Even with the better quality greenhouses, there is never enough. Be specific when you make your order. Ventilators should be positioned both in the roof and on the sides. Roof vents provide gentle air movements and should be opened first. In warmer weather the side vents are used in conjunction, to bring cool air, while the hot air is expelled through the roof. In winter, you need to have, as a favourite old phrase would have it, a 'buoyant atmosphere'.

The heaters are used to create air movement, assisted, if possible, by fans. It is always better to over-ventilate than stagnate. A fan will ensure there are no cold pockets or hotspots and significantly reduce fungal problems.

Remember, an unattended greenhouse on a hot day is potentially as damaging as an unguarded, cold and frosty night.

Whatever form of heating you choose, it should be thermostatically controlled. Most plants only need to be kept frost free, and a thermostat set to 3°C/37°F in a well-insulated greenhouse will not need to kick in very many times in the average winter. If you are setting your temperatures higher, fuel cost may be a consideration (if so, why are you setting your temperatures higher? Bring the shiverers into the house!). In which case gas is marginally cheaper than electricity, at the moment of writing. Bubblewrap will cut your heating bill, but also cut the amount of light coming in. Don't forget to plug any leaks in your greenhouse and ensure that doors shut properly.

▼ A single layer of bubblewrap is enough to cut the heating bills without cutting out too much light coming in, which the tender grasses and begonias need.

COLD FRAMES

Cold frames are much underestimated. They can be versatile and so much can be achieved using them without the need of a greenhouse. Most are permanent, made of wood or of concrete blocks. They can also be temporary, made out of straw bales or blocks moved into place for the winter. This is snug but a nuisance.

Solid concrete blocks can be thin and save space but the hollow ones provide more insulation. Wood is easy to handle and to assemble but it doesn't have the insulating properties of concrete and doesn't last as long.

If your frames are temporary and merely for providing protection at winter's end, they can be taken away, having done that duty, and stored. But if permanent, you'll be using them throughout the summer for a succession of propagations. They needn't stay empty for long from seed sowing through to root cuttings.

▶ The nursery and potting shed, with the long cold frames for saleable plants. Behind the scenes are more cold frames, which we use in every season, in spring to raise and harden off seedlings and for establishing newly potted, rooted cuttings taken off soft perennials in autumn—fuchsias, felicias and such like. In May the frames are valuable for annuals, such as ipomoeas, zinnias, and for late sowings of cosmos, annual rudbeckias and dahlia seed strains. We also put dahlia and canna tubers in the cold frames when they come out of winter storage to start them into new growth. We bed them into old, moist potting compost and keep the frame closed, but shade it if the sun is hot. Then, in autumn, nearly all our display pots containing bulbs are placed in a cold frame, where the amount of rain they receive can be controlled, and they will often remain there until just bursting into flower. The frames also offer protection to many potted plants in winter.

Frames can be sunk or be above ground. If sunk, they retain far more warmth. They can be double-layered or single. We use double-layered frames for most of our propagation. The top must be sloping, to throw off the rain. The lower layer is horizontal. This retains moisture. Water drops hang suspended on the underside.

The cover on top of your frame can be glass, plastic, polycarbonate sheeting or horticultural fleece. In very cold climates, such as winter in much of the USA, a heating element can be used to keep the frames frost-free, using a thermostat to control activation. In cold weather here, we drape horticultural fleece over the top, to provide extra protection.

Ready-made frames can be bought through horticultural mail-order catalogues, but the height of plants being stored is limited. You can even buy TENT frames made of see-through plastic that zip up the front. They are about 1.5m/5ft high and 1.2m/4ft across, with two or three shelves. These are flimsy but of certain use.

Cold frames can be ventilated by slipping the glass on and off, or by blocking the glass up. In summer, shading the glass or wetting the frames inside and out will help to reduce the temperature and stop things overheating. There is a particular danger with children and glass.

WINDOW SILLS

Plants can be kept on window sills or in the room, always with danger from draughts. Traditionally, the bathroom is a good place because of its high humidity. Cellars are frost-free and good for storage if the temperature is level and cool. The same proviso applies to a shed or garage. They can be used for dahlias and cannas stored dormant.

Every year there will be unexpected losses, sometimes our own fault, and sometimes through circumstances we could never have planned for. You just have to be stoic about this; learn the lesson and forge on.

Mary Keen

POSTSCRIPT: TROPICAL HAS BECOME A CLICHÉ

When Christo sacked his mother's roses years ago and replaced them with bananas and other weird and un-English plants, I loved it. It made me laugh out loud to see the dahlias bouncing about with the cannas and bananas.

IN THOSE DAYS neither dahlias nor cannas were socially acceptable and only dukes grew bananas—indoors. A combination of shocking pink, scarlet, mauve and orange flowers flanked by phormiums and zebra-striped grasses was about as rare as a humming bird in Piccadilly. Now gardens are full of Lloydian gusto and it is exhausting seeing clashing half-hardies, much less well grown than at Dixter, in everybody else's patch.

He always reproved me for saying that he was colour crazed; he once said in a letter: 'You mustn't get the idea that I like bright colours—red and orange in particular—only. I like *all* the colours at one time or another.' But he did like playing the *enfant terrible*. The outrageous ties he wore—violet and yellow, or emerald green—seemed to me a sign that he aimed to provoke. Did he change the rose garden as a tease? Or did he think of it as just another brainwave, to enjoy until he had a better one? Once he gave me a dahlia called 'Chimborazo' (vermilion with a gold centre) solely because he thought I would dislike it. We had to look up the poem where the name occurred (*Romance* by W. J. Turner). I still grow it, with marigolds of the African sort which he also favoured. Marigolds, for goodness' sake, I think he started that trend too. They were despised for years and are still rather frowned upon. I get some visitors to the garden who look the other way when they reach my orange corner. He, of course, would have sneered at my lack of bravery. Crocosmia, marigolds and sunflowers with a touch of blue would have seemed a bit cautious to him. Contrast, rather than toning, was more his style.

JUNGLE FEVER

He was always adventurous and he had the space to experiment at Dixter, so he constantly pushed at the boundaries of horticulture. The rest of us slavishly stuck with his last flamboyant scheme, as he moved on. Ten years after he pioneered tropical, did he know what the consequences would be?

In south London, a friend says, you can't walk down a street of Victorian terrace houses without spotting bananas and grasses in the front garden. Jungle fever has broken out from Aberdeen to Cornwall. Every designer now does exotic. Roses or pastel shade borders are so over, that magazines rarely picture them. About grasses he was a bit ambivalent. I seem to remember that the Oudolf border at Wisley got the thumbs down from him for its lack of gusto and its brown colour scheme, so I can't blame Christo for all the grasses grown in gardens now. But I do wish his influence was not so persistent. The originality of schemes that he and Fergus dreamed up at Dixter does not translate well to everyone else's patch. An exotic corner like the rose garden needs to be contained for a start; a place that you visit for a shot in the horti-cultural arm for a few months and then leave to look at something else. If tropical is the only idea in a small garden, it loses its power to surprise, as his patch always did. Besides, he was always changing the plants and finding new ones to introduce. The old rose garden, in its tropical phase, had a fresh look every summer.

I say 'phase' because I think that Christo might have changed it radically before too long. I can't think of him as conservative. Reform was more his style than respect for the past, but I despair about pinning him down, because one of the great things about him was his unpredictability. He would probably reprove me for labelling him a revolutionary and remind me that some traditions at Dixter were sacred. All I want to say is that people who try to copy his style never seem to move on as he was constantly doing.

I am as guilty as any of being influenced by his taste. He introduced me to begonias with Dragon Wing Red ('Bepared') — coral red and dangling and, once I saw the point of Dragon Wing Red, I started to look at other begonias. Now *B. fuchsioides, B. scharffii* and *B. sutherlandii* 'Papaya' — all first seen at Dixter, are regulars in my own garden (clients are harder to convince). I bet I grow them for ever now and probably in the same place — in that little yard behind the kitchen. *Ageratum houstonianum* 'Blue Horizon' is another plant I would never have dreamed of using, unless he had shown the way. It means parks' edging to me, but seeing this taller form threaded through

the borders in his sunk garden made me want to grow it everywhere, but he never convinced me that spotty laurel was as lovely as he made it out to be. He championed aucuba out of, what I suspect was, perversity.

NEW IDEAS

Being original was always Dixter's mission statement, but that is not the message Christo's followers receive. Imitation is, of course, the sincerest form of flattery and he was not averse to that, but here we are faithfully making mixed borders the way that he showed us fifty years ago in *The Well Tempered Garden*. Does anyone make a shrubbery now? And how few people do pure herbaceous, thank to his edicts and example? Tropical has become a cliché. Do you remember when all any gardener wanted was roses up apple trees, inspired by Vita Sackville-West at Sissinghurst? But Christo started so many fashions. Everyone wants a meadow these days — without the meticulous management that he instructed, so messy grass is mostly what we get. Succulents were his final craze, and I wonder if they will influence gardeners in the same way as the re-vamped rose garden did?

People take time to absorb new ideas. 'All taste is retrospective' is a quote that applies to most of the world, but never to Lloyd who, I suspect, preferred the shock of the new. We ought to try to be as original and experimental as him. Slavish following of the fashions that Christo set, without the standards of growing and experimenting that he insisted on at Dixter, mean that we are suffering from an excess of poor pastiche. And far too many tropical schemes.

◀ **Shocking pink** Salvia involucrata 'Bethellii', a tuberous-rooted, nearly hardy perennial sage, is daringly combined with the Collerette dahlia 'Chimborazo'—deep crimson-red 'petals' with a contrasting yellow collar flecked with red. In Succession Planting, Christo admitted, 'This partnership may not be to everyone's taste, but I like my bedding to be full of buzz.' The dahlia is named after the ancient volcano in Ecuador that inspired W. J. Turner's Romance:
'When I was but thirteen or so
I went into a golden land,
Chimborazo, Cotopaxi
Took me by the hand.'

DIRECTORY OF EXOTIC PLANTS

▲ *Abutilon megapotamicum*
Height and spread: to 2m/6½ft
Sun (Z9)
This half climbing, half shrubby trailing abutilon from Brazil needs the protection of a wall. The pendent, bell-shaped flowers are borne from summer to autumn—exactly when needed.

Acer negundo 'Flamingo'
Height: hard prune each winter
Spread: prune to taste
Hardy, best in shade to prevent leaf burn (Z3)
Think of this maple as a flower arranger's dream and forget about it being a variegated apology for a forest tree. Seen at Dixter in a brilliant combination with *Canna* 'Erebus'.

Aeonium 'Zwartkop' ▶
Height: 90cm/3ft
Spread: 30cm/12in
Tender, sun (Z9)
Fat rosettes of shiny purple-black leaves wilt in hot sun, which surely contradicts the whole point of a plant having

succulent foliage in the first place. Apparently the way to keep succulents trim is to stop them flowering and becoming leggy. Propagate by cuttings, using a sandy mixture. Keep frost-free, water sparingly in winter.

Agave americana 'Marginata' ▶
Height and spread (foliage): 90cm/3ft
Tender, sun (Z9)
A big spiky plant excellent for giving solidity to a lax piece of planting and transporting you back to your first Mediterranean holiday. Will live for a long time in the same pot, which can be sunk in gravel for summer and lugged out in autumn to a frost-free greenhouse or bright shed. Keep the pot and centre of the plant dry in winter. Fergus is experimenting by leaving one or two plants outside. Careful positioning is required, as the fierce spines on the tips of the leaves are a grandmother's nightmare—a hazard for children and passing dogs.

Aloe striatula
Height: 1.5m/5ft
Spread: 90cm/3ft
Sun (Z8–9)
An excellent aloe that is also one of the hardiest. A hard winter can drive it underground, but a succession of mild years allows it to make a multi-stemmed shrub. Easy from cuttings. Also look out for **A. mitriformis**, *right*.

Amaranthus cruentus ▼
(syn. *A. paniculatus*)
Height: 90cm/3ft
Spread: 30–45cm/12–18in
Half-hardy annual, sun

Upright velvety flower tassels and leaves deeply suffused with crimson red, a close relation of love-lies-bleeding **'Foxtail'**, *below*, is taller (1.2m/4ft). Sow seed under glass in April or the beginning of May and grow in full sun and well-drained soil.

Amicia zygomeris ▷
Height: 2m/6½ft
Spread: 90cm/3ft
Tender, sun (Z9)
A trouble-free drought-resistant Mexican shrub with beautiful blue-green pinnate foliage, a long succession of yellow pea flowers and funny-looking plump purple-suffused stipules, asking to be squeezed. On a warm site, especially if mulched in autumn, this behaves like an herbaceous plant, renewing itself from below ground each spring. Easy from autumn cuttings.

Aralia elata
Height: 4m/13ft
Spread: 2m/6½ft and suckering
Hardy (Z4)
Feathery umbrellas, most fashionable in the variegated forms, provide distinct shape and movement at a level that is often amorphous in plants of similar stature. The cream flower panicle makes for a last gush of excitement over the fountain of leaves in autumn. Thorns bespeckle the plant throughout.

▽ **Arundo donax**
Height: 3.6m/12ft
Spread: 90cm/3ft
Hardy, sun (Z7)
A terrific, tall reliable plant spreading very slowly, although

in warm climates it can be invasive. Enjoys moisture. Grown in an old cattle-drinking tank at Dixter, it can be watered to suit. Cut down the old stems in spring, and propagate if necessary by dividing up with a sharp spade.

▽ **Arundo donax var. versicolor**
Height: 3m/10ft
Spread: 90cm/3ft
Tender, sun (Z9)
The variegated arundo grown at Dixter has sparkling white banding. More tender than the species, this is best potted up and kept under glass for winter.

Astelia chathamica
Height: 75cm/30in
Spread: 90cm/3ft
Hardier than people think, sun or part shade (Z8)
Protected at Dixter in cold weather with a plastic overcoat stuffed with fern fronds, this native of the Chatham Islands has shining silver leaves, much loved by grazing snails, which spoil the surface of the foliage by creating dark green patches.

Astilboides tabularis
Height: 80cm/32in
Spread: 1.5m/5ft
Hardy (Z3)
Foliage plant requiring moisture, either atmospherically or basically. Beautifully structured leaves that turn to transparent butter in autumn.

Bassia scoparia
Height: to 80cm/32in
Spread: 25cm/10in
Sun
One of the few annuals grown solely for foliage, the summer cypress resembles a bright green dwarf conifer. Also known as the burning bush on account of its reputation for brilliant autumn colour. Sow early April.

Beschorneria yuccoides
Height (foliage): 90cm/3ft
Spread: 2m/6½ft
Sun (Z9)
Relaxed long leaves, tinged with silver, make an irregular mound. The inflorescence surges out as an astonishing pink bud that extends to a 2.5m/8ft arch with green bells on.

Begonia boliviensis
Height: 90cm/3ft
Spread: 60cm/2ft
Tender, shade (Z10)
This tuberous begonia, with bright orange-red flowers is a good summer-flowering plant, with stiffly erect succulent branching stems, which can become lax and may need staking. Tuberous-rooted
B. 'Flamboyant', *right,* (40cm/15in) is generous with yellow-centred small scarlet flowers. This well-loved old cultivar had been dying out due to disease but virus-free plants are now becoming available.

Begonia 'Burle Marx'
Height: 90cm/3ft
Spread: 60cm/2ft
Tender, shade-loving (Z10)
Heavily textured leaves of light and dark green streaked with brown on a good strong plant that rarely needs staking. Also rhizomatous, B. 'Marmaduke' is smaller (45cm/18in) with large leaves handsomely blotched in a mosaic of lime-green and deep reddish brown.

▼ **Begonia Dragon Wing Red ('Bepared')**
Height: 50cm/20in
Spread: 45cm/18in
Tender, shade (Z10)
A semperflorens-type of begonia with fibrous roots, closely related to the dumpy types that colonize every garden centre from Dublin to San Francisco, but a bit less blobby. Red flowers and shiny green leaves illuminate the shady places among taller plants.

Begonia grandis subsp. evansiana
Height: 30–90cm/1–3ft if given sufficient summer heat.

Hardy, dappled shade (Z6)
A genuinely hardy and soundly perennial tuberous begonia. The leaves are small but fresh, and the flowers welcome in an unobtrusive way.

Begonia luxurians
Height: 1.2m/4ft
Spread: 60cm/2ft
Tender, shade (Z10)
This glorious Brazilian, the palm-leaf begonia, loves humidity and shade. The fingered deep green leaves and huge clusters of creamy flowers curl up in sun and drying winds. When comfortably settled under glass you can practically see this jungle

giant grow. Root by tip cuttings (stand these in water for 48 hours before putting them into the cutting mix). Other good shrub-like begonias include: 'Little Brother Montgomery' (90cm/3ft); B. metallica, the metal leaf begonia (90cm/3ft); and B. scharffii (syn. B. haageana) (60cm/2ft).

▼ **Blechnum fluviatile**
Height and spread: 60cm/2ft
Hardy except for coldest parts of the UK/shade (Z8)
Australasian shade- and moisture-loving fern with sterile fronds, 20–85cm/8–33in long with almost round, dull green

leaflets. These lie nearly horizontal, forming a rosette. This fern can form narrow trunks up to 50cm/20in tall. The fertile fronds stand erect from the centre of the rosette and are dark brown and spiky. **B. gibbum** (90cm/3ft), *above*, is a tender and highly desirable miniature tree fern from Fiji which is kept in a pot at Dixter and sunk into the ground for the summer.

▲ *Bougainvillea glabra*
Height and spread: 12m/40ft, but much less in pots.
Tender, sun (Z9)
The typical magenta bougainvillea, a colour Christopher adored. Many of the best Dixter container groupings include one or more pots of this showy Brazilian climber.

Calopsis paniculata
Height: 1.5–2m/5–6½ft
Spread: 1.5m/5ft
Half-hardy evergreen (Z9)
This restioid from South Africa is very upright and similar to a small bamboo, with finely branched stems and grass-like flowers in autumn. Both architectural in the garden and great in flower arrangements. Grow in a well drained but moisture-retentive soil that is on the acid side of neutral.

▲ *Canna* 'Erebus'
Height: 1.8m/6ft
Spread: 50cm/20in
Tender, sun (Z9)
Large blue-green leaves and salmon pink flowers look good mixed with other pinks at Dixter such as the variegated cream and green leaves and pink young shoots of *Acer negundo* 'Flamingo'. After frost or early November, whichever is the first, lift cannas and store in a frost-free shed. Inspect regularly to make sure they haven't become too dry. Bring them on under glass in spring and divide them in late spring or early summer when the soil warms up.

Canna 'General Eisenhower' ▶
Height: 2m/6½ft
Spread: 60cm/2ft
Tender, sun (Z9)
Broad, bronze leaves take on beautiful curves, like a piece of

sculpture, and are crowned by large, intense red flowers. Dead-heading cannas is a good excuse to have a look round the garden every day—just tug off any faded flowers that are spoiling the effect. *C. indica* 'Purpurea' (1.8m/6ft), vigorous, purple tinted, with small orange-red flowers, is a good mixer because the whole effect of the leaves and stalks is comparatively slender. Another with purple-bronze leaves is *C.* 'Wyoming' (2.2m/7ft), seen at Dixter complementing the lighter bronze of the foliage of

Dahlia 'David Howard'. (Could it be that too many gardeners are copying this ensemble?)

▼ *Canna* 'Musifolia'
Height: 3.6m/12ft
Spread: 60cm/2ft
Tender, sun (Z9)
The well-named banana-leaved canna is one of the tallest, with huge wavy leaves edged in maroon on maroon stems. It seldom flowers in our climate and the flowers are insignificant anyway.

▲ *Canna* 'Phasion'
Height: 1.5m/5ft
Spread: 50cm/20in
Tender, sun (Z9)
This tropical beauty (sometimes known as Tropicanna or 'Durban') looks amazing with the light behind it, shining through the stripy cherry-red and purple leaves, with orange flowers atop. You can see why it has three names; everyone would like to be responsible for naming such a high glamour plant. Another canna that looks its best seen against the light is 'Striata' (syn. *C.* 'Malawiensis Variegata'), with translucent upright green and cream striped leaves and silky orange flowers.

Clematis 'Madame Julia Correvon'
Height: 4m/13ft
Spread: 90cm/3ft
Hardy, sun or shade (Z5)
Blessed by being a Viticella, this clematis isn't likely to be attacked by wilt. Any messy growth can be cut back in winter. (You may need to look over the plant again in spring and prune to a healthy shoot.) Madame Julia can drape her small wine red flowers with cream centres over the nearest shrub, head off towards the roof, or, as at Dixter, be trained to climb up a pole. **C. 'Marcel Moser'**, *right*, is a large-flowered hybrid, rosy mauve with a deep carmine bar. At Dixter it grows up a post supporting the hovel roof.

Colocasia esculenta ▶
Height: usually 90cm/3ft, more under tropical conditions
Spread: 60cm/2ft
Tender, sun (Z10)
Commonly known as elephant's ear, this tuberous plant of the arum family has dramatic, dark-green leaves capable of growing to 60cm/2ft long. Makes an excellent pot plant if given warmth and shelter over winter and is worth trying outside in favoured coastal areas.
C. esculenta '**Black Magic**', *far right*, has silky black leaves, brilliantly displayed at Dixter accompanied by the bright variegation of *Arundo donax* var. *versicolor* and cream and green variegated plectranthus. Protect under heated glass in winter.

Cordyline indivisa
Height: 6m/20ft
Spread: 2m/6½ft
Hardy, sun (Z9)
Away from coastal and other-wise climatically favoured areas, it may be worth trying to grow this eminently desirable plant in a tub. You can always ingratiate yourself with the Cornish by donating it to them when it has outgrown your orangery.

Cortaderia richardii
Height: 3m/10ft
Spread: 1.5m/5ft
Hardy, sun (Z7)
More elegant and less thuggish than *C. selloana*, this plant could yet redeem the reputation of the pampas grass.

Cosmos bipinnatus Sonata Series
Height and spread: 90cm/3ft
Although on the short side for a cosmos, this Series has the advantage of coming into flower in good time. As a filler, the feathery foliage never dominates, making it ideal for following perennials which are past their best but need to carry on growing nonetheless.

Cotyledon orbiculata
Height and spread: 30cm/1ft
Tender, sun (Z9)
Attractive succulent, elegantly called pig's ear, with powdery light silvery blue leaves easily grown in extra well-drained mix and a shallow clay pot. Keep virtually dry and frost free in winter. Propagate often to ensure nice compact plants. Succulents look good grouped together in full sun—cotyledons, echeverias, sedums, aeoniums, agaves and so on.

Crassula capitella 'Campfire'
Height: 20cm/8in
Spread: 30cm/12in
Tender, sun (Z9)
Unassuming when happy, this small green succulent turns an astonishing shade of red under stress. There's a fine line between being nice enough to encourage it to grow and beastly enough to make it worth looking at.

Cuphea cyanea
Height and spread: 60cm/2ft
Tender, sun (Z10)
Small shrubby plant from Mexico with pink tubular green-tipped flowers with what looks like two funny black eyes perched on top. Here's looking at you, kid!

▲ *Cyperus papyrus*
Height: 2.5m/8ft
Spread: 90cm/3ft
Tender, sun (Z10)
This tender sedge with all
the ancient connotations of
Egyptian papyrus makes a
graceful addition to summer
plantings. Tall, slender green
stems sway around, each topped
with a mop-like grassy hairstyle.
You can stand the pot in shallow
water in summer then shift
it to frost-free conditions in
autumn (but it can be difficult
to overwinter). Apparently easy
from seed.

▼ *Dahlia* 'Grenadier'
Height: 1.2m/4ft
Spread: 90cm/3ft
Tender, sun (Z9)
With neat, fully double, glowing
red flowers, 'Grenadier' is one
of the really good red dahlias.
Other reds at Dixter include:
D. coccinea (1.8m/6ft) with single
red flowers, tilted downwards;
'**Wittemans Superba**', a
sumptuous red with a button-
like centre which shows a
purple reverse to the small rays
composing it; 'Alva's Doris'
(1.2m/4ft), a Small Semi-cactus
type; and '**Bishop of Llandaff**'
(1.5m/5ft), with single red
flowers and ferny, nicely cut
bronze foliage, so you don't
get the usual wodge of dull
green typical dahlia leaves.
The flowers look best when
they've just opened and the
centres are sumptuous deep
red before they age to yellow.
It is a very popular dahlia and
perhaps, like all celebrities,
may now be suffering from
overexposure.

▼ *Below, clockwise from left*:
Dahlia 'Grenadier';
D. 'Wittemans Superba';
D. 'Bishop of Llandaff'

▲ *Above, clockwise from top left*:
Dahlia 'David Howard';
D. 'Davar Donna'; *D.* 'Glorie van
Heemstede'

▲ *Dahlia* 'Glorie van Heemstede'
Height: 1.4m/4½ft
Spread: 60cm/2ft
Tender, sun (Z9)
This bright yet kindly yellow
dahlia is the most popular of all
Waterlily types. '**Davar Donna**'
(1.4m/4½ft) is a lemon-yellow
Medium Semi-cactus dahlia,
with mid-green foliage and
flowers 13cm/5in across. The
flowers of 'Moonfire' (1.2m/4ft)
are two-tone in deep yellow
fading to orange red in the
middle and the foliage is
bronze. '**David Howard**'
(1.8m/6ft) is a neat, Miniature
Decorative of cheerful, apricot-
orange colouring and, having
dark leaves, is one of the best
garden dahlias.

Echeveria 'Elegans' ▶
Height and spread: 10cm/4in
Tender (Z10)
Echeverias come in an infinite variety of colours and textures, and it is worth trying any you come across (they, obligingly, root from a detached leaf). 'Perle von Nürnberg' is a particularly rewarding shade of glowing, satiny puce. Absolute drought is required in the winter months.

▼ **Ensete ventricosum**
Height: indefinite
Spread: 1.2m/4ft
Tender, sun or shade (Z10)
The Abyssinian banana, native of tropical Africa, has huge olive-green leaves, up to 3.6m/12ft long, with bright red midribs. Nothing could be better for instant tropical effect, but it does require winter protection in a warm greenhouse.

Escallonia bifida ▶
Height and spread: 3m/10ft
Hardy in warmer areas, sun (Z8)
The beauty of an otherwise plain

▲ *Above, clockwise from top left*: *Dahlia* 'Hillcrest Royal'; *D.* 'White Ballet'; *D.* 'Pearl of Heemstede'; *D.* 'Fascination'

▲ **Dahlia 'Hillcrest Royal'**
Height: 1.5m/5ft
Spread: 90cm/3ft
Tender, sun (Z9)
Near the top of Christopher's list, '**Hillcrest Royal**' is a spiky Medium Cactus of brilliant purple (not quite magenta) colouring. Collerette *D.* 'Chimborazo' (90cm/3ft) is one of the more challenging dahlias to position from a colour point of view—deep crimson outer petals and pale yellow, red-flecked prominent middles. Pinkish purple '**Fascination**' (80cm/32in) is a Peony-flowered type with dark bronze leaves. Clear pink '**Pearl of Heemstede**' (1.2m/4ft) is a Small Decorative type, with rounded petals. '**White Ballet**' is a Waterlily dahlia of similar size, more ivory than white.

Dicksonia squarrosa ▼
Height: 2–6m/6½–20ft
Spread: 3m/10ft
Tender, shade (Z8)
This beautiful New Zealander needs moist air and protection from strong winds and frost. Just what you want for instant impact if you can offer this wonderful fern the conditions it needs. *D. antarctica* (3m/10ft) is the easiest and most widely available tree fern, but it too needs shade, shelter and humidity (you will probably need to protect the crown in the cold months and supply extra moisture in the warm).

family, most of which have an angular, somewhat moth-eaten habit. In September in the Exotic Garden, this presents a great mass of starry white flowers, beloved of butterflies.

▶ *Eucalyptus gunnii*
Height: 2m/6½ft (stooled)
Spread: 75cm/2½ft
Hardy, sun (Z8)
Stooling the cider gum has long been practised at Dixter: plants are cut down to a stump each spring, thus ensuring that juvenile foliage—with pretty rounded leaves, as opposed to the longer adult leaves—continues to be produced. The light powder-blue foliage offers excellent contrast to purple-leaved plants. Young eucalypts don't enjoy being stooled indefinitely, so at Dixter fresh seed-grown plants are readily available. *E. perriniana*, *top right*, the spinning gum, is distinctive because each pair of leaves is joined to form a perfect disc around the stem.

▼ *Eupatorium capillifolium*
Height: 1.2m/4ft or more
Spread: 30cm/12in
Tender, sun (Z10)
At first glance this looks like a giant, bright green hairy caterpillar. It forms slender columns of grass-like foliage and is used as a colour separator in the Dixter borders.

Euphorbia cotinifolia ▶
Height: 1.5m/5ft
Spread: 90cm/3ft
Tender (Z10)
Heartbreakingly tender and difficult to get through the winter. Glamorous dark foliage on a plant that is not easy to identify as a spurge, should it survive more than five minutes in your greenhouse. Also tender, is the evergreen honey spurge, *Euphorbia mellifera* (2.5m/8ft), *far right*, with lush green foliage. Hardy *E. donii* (1.5m/5ft) is clump forming with smart, lime-green flowers from July to October.

Fascicularia bicolor
Height: 30cm/12in
Spread: 60cm/24in
Hardy (Z7)
Happy in shade, this bromeliad is grown in the gutter on the north side of the house at Dixter. Val Dillon calls it the Monkey's Bottom Plant, which gives some indication of the flower colour.

Fatsia japonica
Height: 3m/10ft
Spread: 2.5m/8ft
Shade (Z7)
Like a giant shrubby ivy, to which it is related, this plant is invaluable for giving the feeling of being in the darkest jungle.

Fuchsia 'Lena' ▶
Height and spread: 30cm/1ft
Hardy (Z7)
Blush white with a fully double rosy magenta centre, 'Lena' starts flowering in late June and just carries on, the stems

arching under the weight of the blossom. 'Mr West' (45cm/18in), with variegated grey-green and cream leaves and pendulous carmine flowers, is one of the best variegated fuchsias and excellent in containers.

Geranium maderense
Height and spread: 90cm/3ft
Tender (Z10)
Monocarpic and tender cranesbill, which makes an almost spherical structure of its glossy leaves above and old stems propping the trunk from below. Soon, or eventually, depending on the growing conditions, it will flower in a fashion so spectacular that it overwhelms and kills itself. Operatic stuff. Used in exotic pots at Dixter, and in the Exotic Garden for foliage effect.

Gunnera manicata
Height: 3m/10ft
Spread: 5m/16½ft
Hardy (Z7)
A single leaf of this plant is a tropical garden in itself. The similar, slightly smaller, *G. tinctoria* holds its leaf in a more perpendicular way, making it more satisfying, architecturally. Inverting the leaves over the crowns in autumn for protection is a nice annual ritual.

181

truffles, intensified at night. The languid white flowers appear in autumn—earlier flowers have usually been destroyed by capsid bugs. Although cut back by frost in winter, will probably reappear in spring.

Ipomoea lobata ▶
(syn. *Mina lobata*)
Height: 2–5m/6½–16½ft
Tender, sun (Z9)
This sweet little tender annual climber has tubular flowers, which mature from red through yellow to white. Mina runs about delicately through giant tropical foliage, like a mouse dancing on an elephant's back. Sown in May at Dixter and used to clamber up other plants.

Ipomoea tricolor 'Heavenly Blue'
Height: 3m/10ft
Tender, sun (Z9)
One of the reasons for getting out of bed before lunch is to see the morning glory in bloom. The flowers collapse at mid-day and overnight it's easy to forget just how heartbreakingly blue they are. This Mexican perennial is usually grown as an annual, sown in May at Dixter for planting out in June. Don't plant the seedlings out too early in summer—after a cold night the leaves turn yellow with resentment.

Kniphofia caulescens
Height: 60cm/2ft
Spread: 60cm/2ft
Hardy, sun (Z6)
Poker, grown mainly for its leaves, which are blue-green

▲ **Hedychium densiflorum 'Stephen'** (*top*)
Height: 90cm/3ft
Spread: 60cm/2ft
Hardy, shade (Z7)
All members of the ginger family are interesting, and surprisingly hardy in temperate gardens. 'Stephen' has fragrant light yellow flowers and orange stamens. *H. forrestii* (1.8m/6ft or more) has notably fresh green foliage. *H. coccineum* '**Tara**' (1.2m/4ft), *above*, is the cream of the crop, with showy bottle-brush deep orange September flowers and especially good bluish-green leaves. Slow to increase unless well fed and watered.

Impatiens tinctoria
Height: 1.2m/4ft
Spread: 90cm/3ft
Tender, shade (Z9)
One of the more glamorous busy lizzies with a seductive scent reminiscent of white

and arranged in a spiralling rosette. Excellent corner plant. *K. linearifolia, below left,* (1.2m/4ft) came to Dixter from Kew and flowers late, but justifies itself by having leaves in a refreshing shade of green all summer. As with all pokers, the essentials for a healthy plant are a good sunny position, no jostling by neighbouring plants and moisture in the growing season.

▼ **Melianthus major**
Height: 2.25m/7½ft
Spread: 2m/6½ft
Evergreen shrub, sun (Z8)
The noblest foliage plant. Divided, serrated leaves provide intricate and bold patterns. The colour is of varying glaucescence. Hardy, with some protection, once established. Treat as herbaceous.

Musa basjoo
Height: 3m/10ft
Spread: 2.5m/8ft
Hardy in recent winters, sun
  (Z9)
Considered the hardiest of all bananas, *Musa basjoo* needs rich soil, moisture and a sheltered position to protect the vulnerable leaves. Palm trees and bananas have to be the two plants that most define exotic gardens. At Dixter a thick padding of fern fronds is used to protect the stem in winter. However, if frosted, the rhizomes may regenerate from below ground in spring.

▼ Opuntia robusta
Height: 3m/10ft
Spread: 1.5m/5ft
Tender, sun (Z9)
This giant prickly pear has great glaucous oval pads set at varying angles, robust enough to carry an annual climber such as *Ipomoea lobata*. Enjoys a romp in the open ground during the summer, if you feel up to manhandling the greatly increased weight back into the greenhouse come autumn.

▲ Paulownia tomentosa
Height: 4.2m/14ft stooled (to 20m/65ft if not stooled)
Spread: 2m/6½ft
Hardy tree, sun (Z5)
Stately Chinese tree with purple foxglove-like flowers when mature. Very often this tree is stooled (cut back almost to the ground in spring, allowing only one or two shoots to develop) thus providing enormous furry leaves, up to 90cm/3ft long. (Allow the plant to establish for two or three years before doing this.)

▼ Pelargonium 'Frank Headley'
Height: 60cm/2ft
Spread: 45cm/18in
Tender, sun (Z10)
A popular old cultivar with cream and green variegated leaves and pale salmon flowers —one of the best for tolerating wet English summers. Cuttings taken in early autumn will bulk up your display for the following year. Pelargoniums prefer a soil-based potting mix. Keep under glass from September until early June.

▲ Pennisetum setaceum 'Rubrum'
Height: 90cm/3ft
Spread: 45cm/18in
Tender, sun (Z9)
This is a beautiful purple-flushed, must-have grass with long-lasting, reddish-beige flowers. Lift the plant in autumn, disturbing its roots as little as possible.

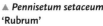

▼ Phlebodium aureum (syn. *Polypodium aureum*)
Height: 90cm/3ft
Spread: 75cm/2½ft
Tender, shade (Z10)
The rabbit's foot fern has creeping rhizomes covered with golden scales, and graceful, steely blue, deeply lobed fronds. It seems to prefer the atmosphere in a house rather than the more humid air of the greenhouse. Easily propagated from spores when ripe.

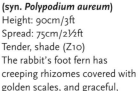

▼ Phormium 'Sundowner'
Height and spread: 1.8m/6ft
Hardy, sun (Z8)
This dramatic New Zealander, wonderfully tolerant of wind and salt spray, makes a brilliant permanent resident of the Exotic Garden, with smart striped leaves of cream, pink and purple. Groom annually with sharp scissors to remove withered leaves from the base. After some years phormiums can become hulking brutes and are heavy work to lift and divide. *P. cookianum* subsp. *hookeri* 'Tricolor' (1.2m/4ft) has lax, arching leaves prettily striped green, pinkish purple and cream; clusters of tubular pale yellowish green flowers are a bonus in early summer. As it hates being moved and sulks for a year afterwards, Fergus simply chops pieces off to reduce its size.

Polystichum polyblepharum ▶
Height: 60–80cm/24–32in
Spread: 90cm/3ft
Hardy, shade (Z5)
This evergreen fern produces shuttlecocks of spreading lance-shaped deep green fronds, slightly lustrous above, and covered with golden hairs as they unfurl. Propagate by division or by ripe spores in summer.

Pseudopanax ferox ▶
Height: to 3m/9–10ft
Spread: 60cm/2ft
Tender, sun or shade (Z9)
Like many Australasian plants, this toothed lancewood has juvenile foliage with sharp narrow leaves to 45cm/18in long that hang at an angle from the straight stem. At this stage the whole plant, a study in brown, looks remarkably dead. After about fifteen years the tree suddenly develops into an

ordinary, mop-headed green-leaved tree with small, rounded, smooth-edged evergreen leaves. *P. lessonii* '**Gold Splash**' (3m/10ft), *above right*, is a New Zealand gem, becoming better known for ease of culture and tolerance of poor conditions and is probably hardier than the books suggest. Lively variegated foliage of yellow and green is equally good in sun or shade. Easy from cuttings, but can take three to four months to root. This member of the ivy family is also amenable to life in a container.

Puya alpestris
Height: 80cm/2½ft
Spread: 70cm/2¼ft
Bromeliad (Z9)
Most exciting when it flowers, in shades of unearthly jade-blue and iridescent with it (think of a peacock's feather).

▼ Rhodochiton atrosanguineus
Height: 3m/10ft
Tender, sun or shade (Z9)
A slender twiner, never too heavy for its host, be it shrub, rose, perennial or more hefty climber. The black-purple flowers, suspended from bell-shaped calyces form a non-stop

profusion of colour from spring until late autumn. Best grown as a biennial, sown under frost-free glass the previous autumn.

Rhus × pulvinata Autumn Lace Group
Height: 2–3m/6½–10ft
Spread: indefinite
Shrub (Z2)
Suckering shrub with intricately divided leaves, green above, bluish beneath clasping red stems. Colours elaborate into the autumn.

▼ Ricinus communis
Height: 2m/6½ft
Spread: 1.5m/5ft
Tender, sun (Z9)
Grown from seed as an annual, this tropical castor oil plant with large palmate dark leaves works as either feature or foil. Requires rich soil and plenty of elbow room.

Rudbeckia triloba ▶
Height: 2m/6½ft
Spread: 60cm/2ft
Hardy, sun (Z5)
A biennial cone flower or brown-eyed Susan, with prominent dark centres and reflexed yellow petals; this is a biennial or short-lived perennial. One of the many late-summer-flowering yellow daisies grown at Dixter, this vivacious American adds charm and vitality to an autumn border. *R. hirta* Cherokee Sunset Group (80cm/2½ft), in shades of bronze, caramel and orange, looks much better in the garden than the photograph in the seed catalogue might suggest.

▲ Salvia involucrata 'Bethellii'
Height: 1.5m/5ft
Spread: 1.2m/4ft
Tender, sun (Z9)
Christopher loved this vigorous, long-flowering, shocking pink, shrubby salvia; it is a really good plant but its brittle stems are susceptible to wind. *S. i.* 'Boutin' looks the same but flowers earlier. *S. confertiflora* (2m/6½ft) has stunning deep red spikes of flower in late summer, on velvety red stems, which provide an excellent climbing frame for *Ipomoea lobata*. Mexican bush sage, *S. leucantha* (90cm/3ft) is more

tender (Z10) but a plant to drool over: the leaves flip to white undersides and the undulating spikes carry flowers of good mauve enhanced by white calyces. *S. splendens* '**Rambo**' (90cm/3ft), *above right*, has red calyces on 30cm/12in spikes that accentuate bright red flowers over dark green leaves.

Schefflera rhododendrifolia (syn. S. impressa)
Height: 6m/20ft
Spread: 1.5m/5ft
Hardy, sun (Z8)
Evergreen tree with fascinating divided leaves, at the vanguard

of a host of species in this genus which have begun to invade our consciousness in recent years. The hardiness of many is attested though still unproved. Look out for forms of *S. taiwaniana*.

▼ Senecio mandraliscae
Height: 20cm/8in
Spread: 90cm/3ft
Tender, sun (Z10)
Seldom seen for sale, but easily propagated from a begged cutting, this composite makes a pool of succulent blue as the season progresses, rooting as it travels.

▲ Setaria palmifolia
Height: 60cm/2ft
Spread: 90cm/3ft
Tender, sun or partial shade
  (Z9)
Achingly desirable grass from tropical Asia with deeply pleated leaves. This acts as a temporary foil among tender perennials at Dixter, where it's potted up to overwinter under cool but frost-free conditions.

Solenostemon (Coleus) hybrids
Height: variable, but below
  90cm/3ft
Spread: variable
Tender, sun or part shade (Z10)
Used to great effect in the hot summers of the US, at Dixter these tender foliage plants with vivacious leaf colours are grown from seed, sown under glass in May. When summer is estab-lished the young plants are bedded out to take the place of faded earlier planting. Especially good colours can be propagated by cuttings.

Tetrapanax papyrifer ▶
Height and spread: 6m/20ft
Tender and suckering, sun
  (Z8–9)
The huge umbrella-like leaves of the Asian rice-paper plant are essential for creating a tropical look. The stems and the backs of the leaves are covered in soft, beige down. It suckers freely, and even if cut down by frost in a harsh winter will regenerate from ground level. There are several good forms of the species available including 'Rex' and 'Steroidal Giant' — need one say more?

▲ Thalia dealbata
Height: 1.8m/6ft
Spread: 60cm/2ft
Hardy, sun (Z9)
The water canna has striking blue-green oval leaves and tall

stems with true violet waxy flowers. Propagate from seed or by division in spring.

▼ Tibouchina urvilleana
Height: 3m/10ft
Spread: 2m/6½ft
Tender, sun (Z10)
Sumptuous rich violet satin flowers appear in succession from August until November but for this tender South American shrub not even a touch of frost is acceptable. Easy from cuttings under glass. If you remember to water regularly, tibouchina works well sunk into the border, pot and all.

▼ Tigridia pavonia
Height: 60cm/2ft
Spread: 30cm/1ft
Hardy, sun (Z9)
These corms make a wonderfully flaunting contribution to the summer garden. Although they last only a day, the flowers are brilliantly gaudy, ranging from white through red to yellow, often spotted or blotched. These iris relatives need a very warm, sheltered, well-drained position.

Trachycarpus wagnerianus
Height: 6m/20ft
Spread: 2.5m/8ft
Hardy, sun (Z8)
One of the hardiest palms, renowned for tolerating cool

conditions, which will give an instant tropical effect. Choose a sheltered position, away from strong winds for this highly decorative, slow-growing ever-green with fan-shaped leaves and dense showy clusters of flowers in early summer. Superior to the better known **T. fortunei**, *above*.

its shapely outline. *Y. whipplei* (30cm/12in) forms a dense rosette of deadly sharp needle-leaves at ground level. Can be left outside in a favoured spot, if you have one (spot or plant) to spare. At Dixter it is grown as a stylite.

▼ *Zinnia* **'Profusion Orange'**
Height and spread: 30cm/12in
Zinnias are thrilling. A good summer helps them along, but is by no means essential. Larger flowers and hotter colours, particularly pinks and oranges make the most tropical effects. 'Profusion Orange' is the best. Fergus sows zinnias at the beginning of May for planting out in June.

Verbena bonariensis
Height: 2m/6½ft
Spread: 30cm/12in
Hardy, sun (Z9)
In the first year of the Exotic Garden at Dixter this was the dominant plant, making a purple haze over what had been the rose garden. Since then it has been carefully controlled, but still makes a theme, albeit a more subtle one. A short-lived perennial. It doesn't self-sow for everybody, but may be encouraged with a little grit and less hoeing.

Woodwardia radicans
Height: 90cm/3ft
Spread: 4m/13ft
Hardy, shade (Z9)
The lounging fronds of this exquisite fern develop embryonic offspring on their undersides, making it easy to propagate. Perfectly happy in a living room in the cold season. *W. unigem-mata* is reputed to be hardier, and as it is not nearly so luxuriant it certainly looks the part.

Xanthophthalmum segetum ▶▶
(syn. *Chrysanthemum segetum*)
Height and spread: 60cm/2ft
Hardy annual, sun (Z7)
The corn marigold made Christopher smile. It is a cheer-ful bright yellow self-sowing daisy with grey-green leaves that lives in all our imaginations with

cornflowers, Shirley poppies and nasturtiums. A good mixer in sunny situations and excellent for picking. Fergus thins seed-lings before they crowd each other out and pulls out plants that turn out to be in the way.

▼ *Yucca gloriosa*
Height: 2m/6½ft
Spread: 1.2m/4ft
Hardy, sun (Z7)
The stiff, sword-like evergreen pointed leaves form handsome

rosettes. A great occasion occurs every year or two when a tall spire emerges from the centre of each rosette, to burst into a carillon of creamy bell-shaped flowers. Choose a well-drained position in sun. In *Y. flaccida* 'Ivory' (1.5m/5ft) a slender inflorescence of creamy white pendulous flowers appears in late summer above a mound of narrow, grey-green leaves; give this evergreen US native plenty of space to display

INDEX

Compiled by Tony Lord.
Page numbers in *italics* refer to illustrations and planting plans.
Page numbers in **bold** refer to principal references. For an explanation of hardiness zones, e.g. **Z9**, see page 191.

Hardiness Zones

Zone	AVERAGE MINIMUM WINTER TEMPERATURE					
	°C			**°F**		
1	below −46			below −50		
2	−46	to	−40	−50	to	−40
3	−40	to	−34	−40	to	−30
4	−34	to	−29	−30	to	−20
5	−29	to	−23	−20	to	−10
6	−23	to	−18	−10	to	0
7	−18	to	−12	0	to	10
8	−12	to	−7	10	to	20
9	−7	to	−1	20	to	30
10	−1	to	4	30	to	40
11	above 4			above 40		

The hardiness zone ratings given for each plant suggest the approximate minimum temperature a plant will tolerate in winter. However, this is only a rough guide, since hardiness depends on many other factors, such as the depth of the plant's roots, the structure of the soil in which it is planted, its water content at the onset of frost, the duration of cold weather, the force of the wind, and the length and heat of the preceding summer. Major conurbations and sheltered sites can be in effect about one zone warmer than the prevailing norm, whereas exposed sites or 'frost pockets' can be one zone cooler.

Contributors

Stephen Anderton
is a writer and broadcaster, a gardening correspondent for *The Times* and author of *Rejuvenating a Garden* and *Urban Sanctuaries*. In his forthcoming biography of Christopher Lloyd, undertaken at his subject's request, Stephen reveals the secrets of a full gardening life.

Tom Cooper
was for 22 years the editor of *Horticulture*, the Boston-based magazine for which Christopher Lloyd enjoyed writing. Tom was a regular visitor to Dixter. He also lectures and writes. He is the author of *Odd Lots*.

Helen Dillon
is a plantswoman, writer, lecturer and broadcaster of world renown. She is the editor of *In an Irish Garden* (with Sybil Connolly) and author of *Garden Artistry, Helen Dillon on Gardening, Helen Dillon's Gardening Book* and *The Flower Garden*. Christopher Lloyd wrote a chapter on her garden in Dublin in his *Other People's Gardens*, which he summed up thus: '[It] has so many delights and over so many seasons that it obviously needs visiting over and over again. I wish I lived nearer.'

Dan Hinkley
plantsman, plant explorer, educator and horticultural consultant, is co-founder of Heronswood Nursery which he operated until 2006. He is author of *The Explorer's Garden, Winter Ornamentals* and *Making Heronswood*. He and his partner retain numerous good memories of times at Great Dixter. On his last trip to the Pacific Northwest, Christopher Lloyd planted a tree in their new garden, Windcli?, near Indianola, WA.

Mary Keen
is a highly respected writer and a leading garden designer. She is the author of several successful books, including *Creating a Garden*, which features the restoration and transformation of her garden in the Cotswolds, which is regularly open to visitors. She writes for *The Spectator* and the *Daily Telegraph*.

Roy Lancaster OBE VMH
is a plant explorer, plantsman, writer, lecturer and broadcaster. His fascination for plants has taken him round the world and he has published accounts of his expeditions in *A Plantsman in Nepal* and *Travels in China*.

Andrew Lawson
is a distinguished garden photographer, a knowledgeable gardener and an expert on colour in the garden. As well as *The Gardener's Book of Colour*, recent works include *The English Garden* (with Ursula Buchan), *Dream Gardens* (with Tania Compton) and *The Elements of Organic Gardening* (with HRH The Prince of Wales).

Tim Miles
is a Cornishman who has been a passionate exotic gardener for many years. Previously at London Zoo and now Head Gardener of Cotswold Wildlife Park and Gardens in West Oxfordshire, he has developed a range of exotic planting styles in and around a diversity of exotic animal species. He is a RHS Committee Member.

Anna Pavord
is a broadcaster and the author of the highly acclaimed *The Tulip* and *The Naming of Names*, as well as *The Flowering Year, The New Kitchen Garden* and *Plant Partners*. She is gardening correspondent for the *Independent*. She travelled to Turkey with Christopher Lloyd to work on *The Tulip*.

Frank Ronan
is a novelist who sometimes commits horticultural journalism.

Ray Waite
is a lecturer, author and specialist in glasshouse plants. Now retired, as Superintendent of Glasshouses at the Royal Horticultural Society Garden, Wisley, he was responsible for the displays of coleus, which Christopher Lloyd admired.

Editor's acknowledgements

Greatest thanks are due to Fergus Garrett, without whom there would be no Exotic Garden at Great Dixter, let alone a book on the subject, and to the Dixter team, in particular Perry Rodriguez, Aaron Bertelsen, Matt Reese and Kathleen Leighton.

Especial thanks to Jonathan Buckley for capturing the excitement of the Exotic Garden in an outstanding set of photographs taken over more than two decades.

Thanks, too, to Audrey Pharo for her help with photographs from the Dixter archives, to Michael Marriott for information on the roses in Lutyens' plan, to Tony Lord for checking everything and compiling the index, to Vicki Vrint for proof-reading, and to Ken Wilson for designing the book and drawing the artworks. Thank you, also, to Viv Bowler, Nicky Ross and Eleanor Maxfield at BBC Books.

As well as the friends who are acknowledged in Frank Ronan's Preface, others who helped Fergus include Greg Redwood, Dennis Schrader and Wayne Winterrowd.

All the photographs are by Jonathan Buckley except those listed below (*l* = left, *r* = right, *t* = top, *c* = centre):
DIXTER ARCHIVES 10*t*, 10*c*, 11*t*, 94*t*, 130*tl*, 130*tr*
ERIC CRICHTON 11*c*

EXOTIC PLANTING FOR ADVENTUROUS GARDENERS

Published in 2007 in North America by Timber Press, Inc.
The Haseltine Building
133 S.W. Second Avenue
Suite 450
Portland, Oregon
97204-3527 USA
www.timberpress.com

A catalog record for this book is available from the Library of Congress

ISBN 978-0-88192-842-6

Designed and typeset in FF Scala Pro by Ken Wilson | point918

Colour separations, printing and binding by Butler and Tanner